LUCKY BREAK

LUCKY BREAK SERIES

HOPE MALONE

ONE

LILY

Strange, but as I look up at the California Bungalow, the word 'charming' no longer fits. Not as it had in the glossy brochure I'd picked up at the realtor's office.

Like a lot of decisions in my life, I'd made it on the spur of the moment. I'd only been after a short-term rental to allow me to escape the motel. I hadn't intended to buy a place.

But something about the house had appealed to me, meaning I hadn't given the purchase the attention it deserved. Heck, I'd given it no thought at all.

Wracked with a crippling sense of guilt and grief, I hadn't been thinking straight.

At the time I'd signed on the dotted line, my sole aim was to take the money I'd inherited from Dolores, my nan, and make good on it. I owed that to my maternal grandmother after she'd raised me from the age of seven, following the loss of my parents and younger sister in a car accident.

But for a nasty stomach bug, I'd have been with them on that day trip, rather than staying with Nanna Dot, to be cosseted and pampered. That was my first guilt.

The second was as good as abandoning my nanna when I went away to college and lost myself to a lifestyle of study and partying. Thanks to those distractions, it had been all too easy to forget the woman who'd raised me.

And now it's too late to follow through on the promises I'd made after I'd started work. Promises to travel up to Coogan's Break so I could spend quality time with her rather than relying on video calls.

Particularly shameful was Mitchell—my ex-husband —and me being in Mexico when she moved into the Rose Haven Retirement Home. I should have been there to help her, for all she said there was no need.

The vacation had been a last-ditch attempt to either rekindle our relationship, or for me to fall pregnant. We—or rather, I—had failed on both fronts.

"Okay, Miss Finnegan, she's all yours." I take a second to realize the realtor is talking to me, forgetting for a moment that I've reverted to my maiden name.

When she drops the keys in my outstretched hand, there's no missing the woman's palpable relief. There's also no missing how quickly she jumps into her car and roars off down the road.

Why do I get the impression this place is less fixer-upper and more puller-downer than she's led me to believe? Of course, if I'd taken the time to actually view the property rather than "Jump at the opportunity of a lifetime!" I might not be so in the dark.

"Chin up, it can't be that bad." My words of encouragement don't get me far after I open the front door.

Unable to cross the threshold thanks to the odor of a home that had evidently belonged to an ardent cat lover, I turn and gulp down fresh air. Blast it, I should have known something was up when the realtor said I could as easily check the place out by viewing their video.

Whoever was behind the camera must surely have been wearing a military-grade re-breather. And while I don't have one of those, I've got a couple of masks in the car. Finally, there is a plus to my old job as a dental hygienist. The other plus will be if I can turn a profit on this flip and any others I take on.

Despite training to be a hygienist, I'd never planned on spending the rest of my working life being confronted with wonky teeth and gingivitis.

I turn back toward the front door. If I'm serious about making a go of this flipping business, then I need to get used to taking on projects others won't go near.

Another sniff of the air and I decide that with this place, it's more a case of CAN'T go near.

With a heavy heart and a deep sense of regret, I straighten my shoulders and try to steel myself for my new future. San Francisco, the city I'd called home for so many years, was now firmly in the past.

The end of my marriage hadn't only put a stop to my dreams of a family, it'd also seen an end to my career. With Mitchell a part-owner of the dental practice we'd both worked at, I'd had to pull up stakes and leave.

I try to push the painful memories of our divorce to the back of my mind, but they linger like a dark cloud, threatening to engulf me at any moment. After a deep breath, I race for the back door of the bungalow, eager to put as much distance between myself and my past as possible.

The journey is far from peaceful, with creaky floorboards and spongy sections threatening to trip me at every turn. When I finally burst into the kitchen, I can't help but marvel at the sheer bleakness of my surroundings.

Despite the overwhelming sense of despair that washes over me, I press on, eager to see what lies beyond the back door. My fingers fumble with the key, and when I finally escape, I'm gasping for air. It's as if I've just broken free of a suffocating trap.

As I stumble onto the small back porch, a wave of dizziness overtakes me, and I clutch desperately at the wrought-iron railing for support. As I examine the crumbling concrete underfoot, I wonder how I could have let things come to this.

My new life looms ahead of me like an impenetrable fog, leaving me feeling utterly lost and alone. Tears stream down my face as I realize this isn't the life that I'd envisioned for myself.

Instead of a happy home and family, I'm facing drifts of cat hair and the prospect of a life teeming with feline companions.

I sink to the bottom step, my head in my hands, worried this will prove to be the total of my new life. A lonely, cat-filled bungalow in my childhood hometown.

And yet, even in the depths of my misery, something catches my eye. Through the overgrown weeds and unpruned citrus trees, I spy something that piques my curiosity.

Despite my misgivings, I can't resist the urge to investigate. I'll risk coming face to face with a container crammed from floor to ceiling with catnip and kitty litter.

I have to traverse the width of the property twice before I spy a track through the vegetation. Thankfully, there's enough of a gap that I won't need to visit the local hardware store to buy a machete.

On making it through the greenery, I soon see that rather than being a container under the large dark green covers, there's what looks to be an Airstream. The stainless skin and rounded lines of the legendary travel trailer are a dead giveaway.

It's only after I've walked around to the other side, I see someone has peeled the corner of one tarp back, revealing a door. At first glance, the trailer appears to be in better shape than the house. It's definitely newer.

Despite it being mostly covered like this, what if there's someone living here? Is this even on my property? There'd been nothing in the literature about this. I knock tentatively on the door before stepping back. I wait a few seconds before stepping forward and knocking again, harder this time.

When there's still no response, I risk peeling the corner of the tarp back a little more and peering through the nearest window. With no sign of life, be it human or feline, I try the door handle, expecting it to be locked, but it isn't.

Even more surprising is that inside, despite being gloomy thanks to the tarps, it's pristine, if a little dated. There's a distinct hint of old lady to the décor, although this might be down to the trailer being vintage. Could it be the previous owner lived out here, giving the house over to her feline charges?

It's the only thing that makes sense, because no-one could live in that house without risking asphyxiation, or a fur ball. A quick sniff of the air confirms the Airstream is also clean and dry.

But could that be because they covered the travel trailer with tarps? Remove them and it will leak like the proverbial sieve. I then shake my head. No, if there was a leak, even a historic one, the place would smell musty, wouldn't it?

As it is, all I can smell is the faintest hint of lavender.

It's only after my eyes have fully adjusted to the lack of light that I spot one of the realtor's business cards on the kitchenette counter. There's no missing the woman's overbite in the photo that dominates the glossy card.

It's a sure sign that the trailer is indeed part of the property, and for the first time in a couple of months, I'm struck by optimism.

It looks as if I'll have somewhere to stay while I undertake the flip after all. Certainly, it'll be a step up from my room at the motel down the road. It'll definitely be quieter.

On folding a beige vinyl concertina door carefully to one side, I discover there's even a bathroom, albeit a tiny one. Offsetting the tight confines of the little room is that it appears as spotless as the rest of the small home.

It definitely smells clean.

This could work, and I can even take the travel trailer with me when I move onto my next flip. It isn't until I've thought this that I realize I'm going for it on the flipping front. I don't care what a challenge it is; I owe it to nanna to invest my inheritance.

It's with a spring in my step that I head back to the main house. It's time I had a proper look at just how much of a bargain this place really is. Even better is that with the place now aired out somewhat, I can take my time, no longer having to hold my breath.

It's all going well until I'm back in the hallway heading for the front door that had slammed shut, presumably because of the wind. I'm reaching for the door handle when my world falls away.

I'm too surprised to scream, only able to manage a pathetic yelp. With nothing substantial to grab hold of, I soon find myself thigh-deep in the hallway floorboards.

It's at this point I thank the universe that the house doesn't have a basement as I'd wished for. If it had, I'd be lying down there in a heap by now. It'll still be no easy feat freeing myself.

I'm working through potential solutions, when something scurries across the top of my sandal-clad feet, and it was no cat. This time, I manage a lot more than a yelp. My screams are a combination of horror at what's down there and hopes of sending the rat and any family members running for the hills.

I'm still in full voice when the front door opens a sliver and my screams jam in my throat. The man is enormous, in more ways than one, with my current elevation having my eyes at junk level. He's also covered in tattoos and got more hair on his head and chin than Mitchell would allow on his entire body.

I'm not used to rough-and-ready men like this, having only dated urbane city types, with my ex a prime example of that. There's nothing polished about this guy, his clothing showing signs of hard work. The fit of his jeans does nothing to hide leg muscles that must surely result from hours in the gym.

The other thing that's interesting is that I don't recognize him from school days. With only one college in the area, if he'd gone there, I'd know him, if only by sight, and he wasn't a sight you'd forget in a hurry.

It's then I notice the logo on his black, fitted t-shirt. Lucky Break Construction? Isn't that the company Alice at the Rose Haven Retirement Home had mentioned?

Actually, mentioned is a misnomer, with her praising the team through the roof, which was ironic given they'd apparently been called in to fix the ceiling in her room. But I hadn't gotten around to finding their number, let alone phoning them. In which case, why then is he here?

"Let me help you." He opens the door as wide as he can without hitting me. After first testing the strength of the boards just inside the door, he reaches down, apparently to help free me.

Now all I want to happen is for the floor to finish swallowing me up. There isn't a chance he'll be able to help me, at least not without hurting his back. I'm struggling to find the words to tell him I'll be okay when he shoves his hands in my armpits and I squeak. I haven't had a man this close to me in months, with my breasts tingling in response to the nearness of those huge mitts.

A moment later I'm being lifted free of the floorboards as though I'm not the curvy girl that I am. Rather than let me go, he wraps his arms tight around me, my body now tingling all over in response to being mashed up against a wall of muscle.

Then, as if suddenly realizing how tight he's holding me, he drops me like I'm hot. This has me staggering back and coming very close to visiting with the rat family in the crawl space.

Thankfully, he reaches out and grabs me again, although this time, he's careful to keep some distance. Not until he's sure I've got my footing, does he release me and step back, giving me an encouraging smile.

And I'm mesmerized.

His teeth are white and straight, their proportions perfect. It's a combination that gives him a textbook wolfish grin, telling me he knows all about flossing. I then revise this assertion, with the glint in his dark green eyes hinting more at oral sex than oral hygiene.

Certainly, there's nothing clean about his gaze as it sweeps my body, leaving me feeling more gloriously dirty than I have in my entire life. And then, just like that, it's over. He lifts his gaze to focus on my face, his eyes now having a shuttered quality to them, leaving me thinking I'd imagined the whole thing.

TWO

TYLER

Being a Wednesday, it's unusual to be packing up this early, but the remodeling job we'd been working on had gone without a hitch. No hidden nasties in the walls, no asbestos, and no plumbing issues, had led to us finishing up a couple of days early.

And I couldn't be happier with our schedule having been relentless for the past six months, and it set to continue for the foreseeable future. Our next job is reconfiguring the Dugan home from top to bottom, with them moving out while the work takes place. With the family due to pack up over the weekend, we won't be stepping foot on site until Monday at the earliest.

I've therefore got a few days to myself. Well, not entirely myself, because I'm conscious I've been neglecting my daughter Zoe since scoring the job as supervisor with Lucky Break.

I'm loading my tools in the back of my truck when Ethan, my boss, saunters over, his phone glued to his ear. On hearing his, "I'll get someone to call over there now," I know I'm not escaping just yet.

After ending the call, he shoves his phone back in his tool belt, before grabbing a pencil and what looks to be a receipt out of the front pouch.

"Sorry, Ty, I'd go myself, but I'm taking Lindsey to the doctors for an ultrasound."

His words, while casual, still evoke a visceral response deep in my gut. Hadn't I said the same thing myself in the past? For all the help, those 'normal' scans had provided after the actual delivery. Not even the doctors saw those complications.

It doesn't matter that it's been nearly five years since I lost my wife. Some days, the memories are fresher than others. Rather than give in to them, I instead watch Ethan as he leans over so he can use the leather of his tool belt as a make-shift desk.

His writing was bad at the best of times, but when jotted on a crumpled slip of paper using a carpenter's pencil in need of sharpening, it's atrocious.

As if sensing this, he says, "It's a potential new job for some woman, Lily Finnegan. Thirty-seven Holder Ave. Apparently she's a friend of Alice, that old lady at the Rose Haven." However, with his mind firmly on his wife's appointment, he adds nothing more before leaving.

On looking up at the house Ethan has sent me to, I'm at a loss. Last time I checked, Lucky Break Construction wasn't in the business of building from scratch.

Which would be necessary here, with the place looking to be ripe for demolition. As it is, I reckon termites might be all that's holding the place together. It's then I remember we don't get them as far north as Coogan's Break, meaning the derelict nature is thanks to age and a lack of maintenance.

It's enough to have me pulling my phone out and searching through my contacts. I don't think twice about calling Alice at the Rose Haven, keen to find out more about the client before I go any further.

As always, the old girl talks at a million miles an hour, bringing me up to date with the home's owner, at least in bald terms. Certainly enough for me to get the lay of the land.

On climbing the steps to the front porch, I'm careful where I put my feet with more rotten boards than is typical in the houses we work on. Likewise, I'm careful when I traverse the front porch, only committing to a step when I know the board will take my full weight.

This is easier said than done with me six-four and built like a tank. Just like my old man, or so I'm told, with mom having long ago trashed any photos of him. As dark as she'd been on him when he took off, this doubtless involved flame and sage.

But it wasn't just physical reminders of her ex-husband that she'd had to ditch when she moved into that duplex. She'd had to get rid of a lot of things.

Unlike the rest of the derelict house, the front door looks to be solid wood. I've not even knocked when screaming comes from just inside. This is a surprise on several levels.

First off, I've fully expected the place to be empty. Second, there's no missing that the woman who's screaming is clearly terrified. It's enough to have me reaching for the door handle, surprised and relieved when it turns and doesn't come off in my hand.

I'm as shocked when I open the door a sliver to see if I can help the woman out. She's still screaming, although the pitch then changes, before ending with a squawk. When I first see her, I'm not sure what sucker punches me the most.

That she's in danger, or that she's gorgeous, with both fighting for supremacy.

"Here, let me help you." I ease a foot inside the door, and once sure the floor will support my weight plus hers, I reach down and lift her free.

In our favor, is the boards she's fallen through are so rotten that they offer little resistance. Unfortunately, she'll still sport some bruises.

With her hard up against me, my arms automatically encircling her to keep her safe. Now I'm wondering who'll keep her safe from me. My body hasn't responded to a woman like this in years, five-and-a-half, to be exact.

It's a memory that has me dropping her like she's hot and her coming close to falling back down the hole in the hallway.

"Oh, I'm so sorry!" This time I'm more careful about how I hold her. Tight enough she doesn't fall, loose enough my cock isn't going all 4th of July on me.

While my smile is supposed to put her at her ease, there's nothing relaxed about her response. She's staring at me like she could eat me, or is it she wants me to eat her? My gaze drops of its own volition, and damn, I like what I see. I always was a sucker for thighs plump enough to suck me in and swallow me whole.

To keep some control over my body, I instead focus on her face. I don't need a complication as gorgeous as this in my life, if only for Zoe's sake. Even with my best efforts, we'd lived in seven different apartments and had a flurry of caregivers by the time she was four.

Then mom retired and eked out enough to put down a deposit on a home of her own. It had been an enormous relief when she'd suggested Zoe go live with her. If it weren't for the size of the duplex, I'd be living with them. As it was, I'd had to close-in the back porch to create a small bedroom for Zoe.

Not only had moving in with my mom given the kid some much-needed stability, it had also made it possible for me to get a better-paying job.

It's one I definitely can't afford to lose by getting myself involved with the client, which is what this woman will be if we take the job. Ethan is adamant we don't mess with any homeowners, having fired guys for this in the past.

The last thing I want to do is mess with my current set-up. With me helping mom with the rent and utilities, my life needs to be steady as she goes for a couple more years, at least.

Only once I have the woman safely across the porch and down onto the front path, do I speak again. Meanwhile, she doesn't appear capable.

"When I stopped out front..." I check the address on the ratty slip of paper I've retrieved from the back pocket of my jeans. "I thought it must be a mistake."

If I've expected this to clear some of the confusion on her face, I'm out of luck. She now appears more confused than ever.

"But what are you doing here? I didn't call you. I hadn't even heard of Lucky Break Construction until this morning." She quiets for a second, before muttering, "Alice, why that..."

Without completing this sentiment, she instead looks up at me. "Well, if you're here, I guess you may as well make yourself useful." She then gestures toward the house with a sweep of her arm.

Another glance in her direction, and I decide it's better for my peace of mind if I focus on the house. "What are your plans for the dum... place?"

Now she's staring at me in the same way as I've been looking at the house. "She's not a dump!" The woman bristles in indignation before continuing. "A lick of paint and she'll be gorgeous by the time I'm done with her. She just needs a little love."

Rather than annoy me, as would usually be the case, all I want to do is laugh. "Lady, I could love this pile of... I could love her every which way but Sunday and she wouldn't have a hope."

It's not until I've said the words that it hits me that this is exactly what I want to do, only not to the house. I take another look at the scrap of paper, but to Lily Finnegan, the dump's proud, if obstinate, owner.

The large breath she takes is telling, although I hold my hand up to stop the arguments in their tracks, before extending it to shake hers. "Tyler Pierce. Is there another way in so I can get a proper look at the place?"

I don't dare tell her that this is so I can confirm we should condemn the place rather than flip it.

I know there's a shortage of properties in Coogan's Break. But whoever sold her this pile of crap should have known better than to offload it to what I'm now guessing is a novice flipper.

As I follow the woman down an overgrown path at the side of the house, I'm having difficulty keeping my eyes up. Lily's ass has a magnetic quality to it. Those are cheeks a man could hang onto when he took his fill. The sway of her hips also has a hypnotic quality to it.

She couldn't be more different to Jade, my late wife, if she tried, and yet my body, okay, my cock, doesn't care in the least. Damn it, if the woman has this effect on me when she's wearing ill-fitting overalls, how would it be if she was naked? In my mind's eye, she's only covered by the waist-length, jet-black curls that tumble riotously down her back.

I haven't given this idea the attention it deserves when my boot catches the edge of a long-forgotten garden ornament hidden in the knee-high weeds.

Maybe if I hadn't been following her so closely, I wouldn't have taken her out when I fell. It could have been worse though, with my reflexes always cat-like despite my size.

A twist of my hips on the way down, and rather than land on top of her, we reverse positions, with me breaking her fall. The only disappointment is that she's facing away from me. This disappointment doesn't last beyond her grinding that peach of an ass into my groin as she attempts to stand.

With the way this is playing out, by the time she's erect, I will be, too.

THREE

LILY

As I struggle to get to my feet, there's no missing the tool poking me in the ass. If I didn't know better, I'd think the guy was wearing a tool belt. Well, he is but only the one mother nature gave him, with my body responding to the current challenge, as it never did with my ex.

Mitchell had sported a wiener by comparison. Even after all these years I can still remember our wedding night, although with no-one to compare him to, it hadn't been obvious just how short-changed I'd been.

I should imagine Candy, his chairside assistant, and the woman who'd replaced me, was ever so disappointed. There's nothing I can do to swallow my smug grin at the thought of what their first time together must have been like.

Her perky blondeness had rubbed salt into the divorce's wound when I'd first heard about her, so I sincerely hope she was disappointed. With my mind clouded with thoughts of the pair, it takes a second to get my bearings when I finally stand.

Tyler looks to be in pain. Surely, I didn't hurt him, courtesy of my ungainly efforts to stand? And yet there's no missing his grimace as he struggles to get to his feet. On second thoughts, a quick peek at his crotch and I can see he's not having trouble standing at all.

This again puts Tyler in stark contrast to 'Sir Mitchell the Slow to Rise', as I referred to my husband when in the bedroom. Although never to his face.

Eventually, Tyler straightens, having me even more conscious of his height and broad shoulders. Next to him, I feel positively petite.

I know it's petty, but comparing Mitchell to Tyler is a balm to my being cast aside because I wasn't able to bear children. As with a lot of other things in our marriage, this too had been my fault.

I'd never had the nerve to ask him to be tested, as he'd insisted I was. Years of his sniping, both at home and at work, had left me too worn down to force the issue.

Now that I'm free of the marriage, my relief is palpable. Strange, but on looking back, I no longer find Mitchell as attractive as I once did.

It's only when Tyler says, "Excuse me?" that I realize I must have been talking to myself again. It was a habit that drove Mitchell up the wall, especially when I was wearing a mask and he didn't have a hope of lip-reading my sotto voce commentary.

Although if I think back on some of my spoken thoughts, this was probably for the best.

"Oh, oh, I'm sorry." As I look Tyler over, I don't bother repeating my mumbled thoughts, instead asking, "Are you okay?"

His brow wrinkles before he can answer. "Am I okay? What about you? Sorry if I hurt you. I blame the fallen angel."

In answer to my confusion, he bends over and wrenches something free of the undergrowth. Only on him holding it aloft do I see it is indeed a small statue of an angel, with wings folded and hands clasped in prayer.

There's no sign the small garden ornament ever sported a halo, a bit like the guy holding it. He props it against the side of the house, and we continue on our way. I'm keen to get his opinion of the place rather than simply the hole by the front door. My initial impression of my new flip is that with the right care, it can truly shine.

The only thing I'm unsure of is the logistics of saving it. The closest I've been to wet rot was falling through the floor earlier. As I walk up the back steps, I'm all too conscious of Tyler right behind me. And when he clears his throat, it's all I can do not to spin around and look at him accusingly.

On him following me into the kitchen, there's nothing to show he's disgusted by how broad I am across the beam. If it had been Mitchell, I'd have heard all about my not being the woman he'd wed.

Meanwhile, Tyler's expression is closed, although my

gut tells me this is to protect him, rather than my feelings.

Unsure what to make of it, I decide it's better for both of us if we instead concentrate on the house. As happens in so many of those home makeover shows, I state the obvious. "This is the kitchen."

Rather than look at me as if I'm an idiot, Tyler smiles broadly. "Yeah, the appliances rather gave it away." He then turns on the spot, taking everything in, before asserting, "We're probably looking at a complete gut job."

Even with my having zero experience flipping houses, I can see there's nothing salvageable, which is a shame. I quite like the olde-worlde look of the cabinets.

"Would it be possible to replace the cabinets with like-for-like rather than having glossy white ones?"

Now it's Tyler's turn to examine me, although I'm unsure what about, or even if he concludes what's obviously puzzling him? "Kinda. Those are solid wood, so if you like them, then we might bring them back to life."

As I peer at the battered woodwork and paint-clogged hardware, I'm unable to stop myself from muttering, "Without resorting to black magic?"

Unlike Mitchell, Tyler catches my words, his laughter booming and full of joy. Soon, I'm smiling as broadly as he is, feeling happier than I have in months.

Here at last was a project even a novice like myself could undertake. What did they call it on those flipping shows? That's right, sweat-equity.

It's when Tyler slides past me to walk into a minuscule dining nook off the kitchen that I decide stripping paint isn't the only way I'd like to get sweaty. It's a thought I bury, wanting to save it for the middle of the night when I can't sleep.

There's also me not having a chance with a man like Tyler Pierce. Nor do I want to risk yet more heartache. Not when I'm only now getting over the bitter divorce.

Heck, it's fresh enough Mitchell still has to buy me out of the loft apartment he'd apparently loved more than me. He'd been furious when my lawyer negotiated a sixty-forty split in my favor, saying his higher income meant he'd paid for almost all our living expenses.

The look on the judge's face when I'd explained I'd been the one to put up most of the money for the place had been priceless. I'd owed it to my late parents to fight for my share.

TYLER

As we walk through the house, I'm having trouble focusing on the task at hand. I don't know what it is about this chick, but I can't keep my eyes off her peach of an ass. Okay, and there are other points of interest, too.

The only plus to starting at the back of the property is that the state of the kitchen desensitized me to what else I'd face. On walking into the bathroom, I soon change my mind.

This is mostly down to me, just about going straight through the floor. If not for the many layers of linoleum underfoot, I probably would have.

This, and a brief sniff, has me backing out of the room and straight into Lily, her breasts mashed hard against my back. While she struggles to put some space between us, I close the door with a boom that resounds in the hallway. "Black mold!"

Next to me, Lily appears dazed, although she soon nods sagely. "Let me guess, a complete gut?"

"I'm afraid so." Even with us having looked at what would be the most expensive rooms in the house to fix, the costs of making the place livable are racking up.

Deciding I can't put it off any longer, I stop and make sure I've got her full attention. This is easier said than done, with the woman looking everywhere but at me. Unsure if this is because she likes what she sees, or she doesn't, I don my professional hat and press on.

"What's your budget?" Usually, I'd be more tactful when asking this, but I don't want to waste Lily's time, or mine. The sooner I finish up here, the sooner I get to spend some time with my daughter.

If I get away soon enough, we can even go for a swim at the beach. I know she loves this, and with my mom deathly afraid of the water, there isn't a chance my girl can go other than with me.

Rather than answer me, Lily is staring off into space. At first, I think she hasn't heard me, then it soon becomes apparent she's frantically working through figures in her head. When she finally answers me, I'm surprised. It's a healthy budget.

"I'm waiting for some other funds to come through, otherwise there'd be more." The tightness of her lips leaves me to wonder exactly where those funds are coming from.

Despite this shortfall, there'll still be enough to do the old girl justice. My less than positive comments about the house to one side, Lily has the right of it. The place has good bones.

The ceilings are high and the windows large, giving the house an airy atmosphere. Although you wouldn't want to breathe too deeply right now thanks to the cats' calling cards in every room.

"We can definitely work with that budget. The only trouble is that we're booked for the next six months, at least."

Finally, I've got Lily's undivided attention, with her now staring up at me open-mouthed. It's an expression that leads to many impure thoughts on my part.

"Six months?!" She then buries her fingers in her gorgeous locks in a manner that has me longing to do the same.

Sheesh, get a grip, would you?

It takes all my concentration to confirm this timing. "We're due to start an extensive project on Monday. But I can at least get some prices through to you for completing the basics."

"The basics?"

Keen to get away, I rattle through the fundamentals. Unfortunately, this includes all the big-ticket items, like a new kitchen and bathroom, and fixing all those rotten floorboards.

"We'll also need to check the foundations. The back of the house is definitely lower than the front. Of course, if you're looking at resale value, then you might think about adding a second bathroom and replacing the roof."

Despite not having inspected it, I know if the rest of the house is this decrepit, then the roof will probably match.

After glancing up at where I'm pointing, Lily darts back along the hallway. Despite her speed, she's careful to keep to the edges where the floorboards are a little firmer. She disappears first into one bedroom, and then another before reappearing in the hallway.

"Come, tell me what you think of this idea?"

Her eyes are alight with excitement and she's having trouble standing still, something that has me on my way to join her. And just like her, I avoid any floorboards that have the potential to see me in the crawlspace under the house.

"What if we took in some of that first bedroom, and then swallowed up that silly little dining nook off the kitchen, and made this into a master suite? Would that be possible?"

It's a suggestion that has me booking it out to my truck to grab my laser tape. Her idea has merit, but whether it'll measure up, I'll need specifics before I can answer that.

A quick measure of the room we're in, the other bedroom, and even the kitchen nook and I know it could work. "I'll cost that up for you, too, but obviously it'll all have to wait until we've got availability."

There's no missing Lily's disappointment at this delay. If she's anything like most flippers, she'll be covering mortgage payments while she waits. And there isn't a chance she can offset this by renting the place out.

"Is there anything I can get on with in the meantime?" She follows this up by briefly picking at the peeling wallpaper next to her.

Her wanting to actually work on the project takes me by surprise. Most of the home-owners we work with prefer a hands-off approach. Even some flippers we've worked with haven't wanted to get involved.

I'm still working my way through a potential punch list for her to work on when my phone rings. A quick look at the screen and I'm relieved to see that it's Ethan, and not my mom, with her mainly ringing me because there's an issue with Zoe.

After greeting my boss, I tell him to hang on, rather than continue the conversation in front of Lily. "I won't be a second." I then edge my way down the hall and around into the dining nook.

"What's up?"

"Yeah, you know the Dugan job? Well, they've just canceled on us. Something to do with his brother not being well. They've said they'll give up the deposit, but this leaves a big hole in the schedule."

Sometimes in life, it's as if the planets have aligned. It's obvious this is one of those times. On finishing the call with Ethan, we've agreed that the next project for Lucky Break Construction is Lily's dump.

However, when she appears at the kitchen door, I reserve my judgment because there will definitely be pluses to this job. I'm just not sure if they're pluses I'm prepared for.

FOUR

LILY

While cherry pie and coffee don't make for the healthiest breakfast, I need them after last night. Unable to move into my silver bullet until the electricity is on, I'd had to endure another night at the motel.

And what a night it'd been. Despite it being a Wednesday, the people in the unit next to mine had decided it was party night. Actually, every night appeared to be a party night for that lot.

With the motel manager unwilling to step in and tell them to shut up, and me not brave enough, as before, I'd ended up pulling the pillow over my head. When

I'd eventually fallen asleep, my dreams had been full of rotten floorboards and Tyler doing his best to fix them, and me.

It was this last that had me waking hot and feverish; the sheets tangled around my legs, and pinning me to the bed as surely as my dream Tyler had. I'm still confused by this, with him nothing like Mitchell. And yet, maybe, that's the point, because being married to Mitchell hadn't exactly worked out well for me.

With the utility company set to sort everything out this afternoon, I'd checked out of the motel, my suitcase and assorted bags in the trunk of my car. To be honest, even with no electricity at the trailer, I'd still have moved out.

I'll take candles and sponge baths any day over people singing drunkenly along to Nickelback at three in the morning.

While I wait on my coffee and pie, I open my laptop and sign into Skye High Pies' free Wi-Fi. I haven't finished checking social media to see what Mitchell and Candy are up to when an email pings its arrival.

I'm surprised to see it's from Tyler, my scalp prickling before the sensation drifts south, despite my doing my best to squelch it. We'll be seeing each other daily, and so I need to get a grip, not be swooning whenever he's near me, even if only electronically.

I'm skimming the contents of the email when a server delivers my coffee and pie. "Let me know when you need a refill, Hon."

She then leaves me to continue reading the email, with me starting again from the top. As I slowly read it, the words sound loud inside my head, the voice a rich and distinctive baritone.

Damn it, when I close my eyes, I can clearly see his beautiful smile. It had been a drawback to being a dental hygienist, a preoccupation with people's teeth.

While Mitchell had beautiful teeth, this was thanks to thousands of dollars of work, whereas with Tyler, I suspect it's all down to good genes.

My eyes still closed, I take my first sip of coffee, with it tasting as good as I remember from yesterday. On opening my eyes, I come close to spitting it out when I spot Tyler standing just inside the door, looking over at me.

It takes all my concentration to swallow and smile in greeting. As he walks to my table, my heart thumps in my chest like there's a helicopter overhead.

On coming to a stop next to the old-school diner style table, he dips his head at my laptop. "Did you get my email?"

Only after I've put my coffee cup down do I answer him, worried I might spill it. "Sure did. I'm just reading through it now." Unable to stop myself, next thing I know, I'm asking, "Would you like to join me?"

He grimaces before replying. "That all depends if you're happy with the estimate for the work at your place."

I'm wondering what that has to do with him joining me for coffee when he continues.

"If you are, the team will need to hustle to have everything ready to start work on Monday. If you aren't, then I've still got some number crunching to do. Obviously, number crunching doesn't take as long as organizing materials, meaning I'd have time for a coffee."

Despite not knowing the man well at all, I get his chattering is thanks to nerves. Whether these are down to my acceptance of the estimate, or me, I don't know. I'm not even sure I want to know.

However, if I've learned one thing over the years working in dentistry, it's how to put the nervous at their ease. "Why don't you grab a coffee and we can go over the figures together?"

It's only once he's nodded his agreement to this and walked up to the counter that I realize this will have me stuck eating cherry pie in front of him. This is never a simple task, with me often ending up with cherry juice running down my chin.

The thought alone is enough to have me signaling the server and asking if she can put the pie in a bag for me to take away. That my request takes her by surprise is clear, as my habit was to eat it while enjoying my coffee.

It's at that moment Tyler turns back up and I can see when comprehension makes itself at home on her face. I guess she's seen it all in her time, with her sweeping the plate up without another word.

If I've surprised Tyler, he says nothing when he sits on the bench seat next to me, rather than in the chair opposite.

On seeing my subtle pulling to the side, he explains, "This will make it easier for us to look at the figures together."

Yeah, and do a complete number on my hearing anything you say.

In the end, it's not as bad as I've expected with Tyler going through the figures professionally and answering all my stupid questions. Despite my having no experience with what's involved in a job like this, this time I'll trust my gut.

It's something I should probably have done when I first dated Mitchell.

There's also the fact Alice at the Rose Haven confirmed it was her who'd phoned Lucky Break on my behalf. She's a fan of the team after they'd fixed the ceiling in her room, with her charmed by Tyler, in particular.

I therefore have no hesitation in telling Tyler that I'm happy for Lucky Break to proceed with the work as outlined. I even reply to his email confirming this in writing.

That done, he's a man on a mission, jumping to his feet and talking about lumber. After a distracted, "I'll see you Monday bright and early," he's on his way.

With no word from the utility company, I decide I may as well visit Alice at the Rose Haven. As well as thanking her for recommending Lucky Break in a roundabout way, I enjoy listening to her stories. I've heard things from her about Nanna Dot that I'd only suspected.

On leaving Skye High Pies, I'm holding two of their famous cherry pies. It doesn't take long to drive to the Rose Haven, as with most destinations in Coogan's Break.

It's funny, but when I was growing up here, I thought Coogan's Break was quite the metropolis. On driving through the gates at the Rose Haven, I decide I like my home town being smaller. San Francisco could swallow a person whole and not bother spitting them out.

My having phoned ahead, Alice is waiting for me in reception, greeting me warmly, and not just because of the cherry pies. Nanna Dot had been a friend of hers, and Alice considers me family, having none of her own nearby.

"Come on, sweetie, we can have coffee in my room. It'll be quieter there, and we can catch up about *things*."

Honestly, the old girl was as good as hopping from foot to foot in her eagerness to see how things had gone with Tyler. As is often the case with older people, her manipulations had been as subtle as a sledgehammer.

Only once she's made us a French press of the 'good stuff', do I rattle through everything that happened. I leave nothing out, knowing from experience with Nanna Dot that it was a waste of time. While some thought the old missed a lot, I wasn't one of them.

If I'd left anything out when catching up with nanna, she'd know, and set to grilling me harder than an IRS agent. That woman had missed nothing. It's no wonder she and Alice had gotten along so well.

By the time I've finished, Alice is beaming, and I can't help but laugh. My laughter soon dies when I face reality.

"Yes, he seems like a nice man, but that's all. And anyway, I've still got things to sort out with Mitchell." For a second, I fall silent. "Because of... It won't be easy finding a man happy to settle for what I can offer."

There's no need to go into further detail, because I suspect Alice already knows. When I'd met with the home's manager after nanna's passing, she'd told me they'd miss Dot, especially Alice, with the pair, "As thick as thieves."

It's a given Alice will be all too familiar with my inability to conceive. It's only with hindsight I see it was this that had devastated me more than the break-up with Mitchell. Could it be his town polish had blinded me all those years ago? Should I have looked deeper than the packaging? I'm busy thinking back on Tyler's, ah hem, packaging when Alice stops my dirty thoughts in their tracks.

"Tyler's wife died after giving birth."

As bald and out of the blue as this statement has been, I drop my pie back on the dainty plate Alice had insisted was necessary. "What?!"

As she tells me what had happened, I don't move a muscle for fear of interrupting. Not usually one to gossip, I instead hang on her every word.

Surely women dying in childbirth was something that happened in third-world countries? But apparently not. While reading all those negative pregnancy tests had been devastating, it must pale compared to what Tyler had faced.

"And the little girl? Where is she now?"

"His mom looks after her, mostly. Meanwhile, he works every hour god gave him, saving up for that girl's college fund." She takes a sip of coffee before continuing. "He's a lovely man. Your Nanna Dot had a bit of a soft spot for him."

The sparkle in Alice's eyes says my nanna wasn't alone in this.

I hug Alice goodbye, having heard everything I need to, and then some. The one upshot of all that intel is that I know Tyler is definitely out of the question so far as romance is concerned.

Not because he's a single dad, but because the last thing he needs is to hook up with someone still mourning a failed marriage. No, as attractive as I find him—there I've admitted it to myself—our relationship will be all business.

And I'm thinking this until I turn into the overgrown driveway at the 'new' place, ready to unload what belongings I have with me. On spotting Tyler dressed only in silky black boxers, I come close to driving into a straggly lemon tree.

"What on earth?" I'm not complaining, just wondering why he's in a state of undress. Damn, the man has a fine body with nothing about it I'd change. Even the tattoos enhance rather than detract.

I'm not usually a fan of tattoos, but on him, they look good. More than that, they look spectacular. Unable to move, I'm still sitting there when he walks over to stand next to my car.

It takes every ounce of my scattered concentration to struggle free of the seatbelt and open the door.

Tyler's grin is sheepish. "Sorry about this." He holds his hands out, and even turns on the spot, displaying cheeks more often seen on male strippers. "I was checking the plumbing when a pipe burst." He falls silent for a second before adding, "I didn't think you'd be here today."

I'm barely aware of popping the trunk, but Tyler notices, watching as it slowly opens. He follows this up by taking a couple of steps in that direction. "Anything I can help with?"

On spotting my suitcase and other bags, he looks at me in surprise. "You can't seriously be moving into this dump? For all we know, there could be asbestos."

It wasn't something I'd considered, and I hope this doesn't prove to be true. Asbestos abatement is expensive, at least it always appears so on those flipping shows. I'd rather spend that money on stainless appliances.

"Not the house. There's a travel trailer out back."

His relief is palpable, although I'm not sure why. "Hang on, I'll just get dressed and I can help you with these."

"Honestly, there's no need."

His face transforms, the grin positively filthy. "No need to help you, or no need to get dressed?"

I can't answer him. And anyway, what are the chances he'd hear me over the clamoring of my ovaries?

FIVE

LILY

Despite most of my things being in storage back in the city, I'm still glad of Tyler's help to get my suitcase and bags out to the Airstream. Even putting aside my propensity to over-pack, I'd collected things of Nanna Dot's that I'd missed when I was up here for the funeral.

While I could have got everything there on my own, it's so much easier with Tyler's help. He's tall enough to lift everything above the undergrowth.

And, even though he's now dressed, there are still pluses to following in his wake. My drooling over him like this, while pointless, isn't something I'm going to avoid completely.

When we break into the clearing that surrounds the Airstream, I rush ahead and unlock the door for him. I still can't believe the realtor hadn't locked it after she'd so obviously put her business card in there. It wouldn't have been hard, with the key hanging on a hook next to the narrow door.

My belongings safely on the ground next to the small steps, Tyler lifts a corner of the tarp as I'd done yesterday. "Wow, she's a beauty. Do you want me to uncover her for you?"

While my immediate response is to say 'yes', I dither. "What if the tarps are there because she leaks?"

Tyler shrugs. "We won't know until we move them. At least that way I can have a better look." He grabs one corner of the topmost tarp. "If it looks a mess, we can always put them back."

What he says makes sense, with me nodding my agreement to this. My head hasn't stopped moving when Tyler drags the first tarp to one side. He soon follows this up with a couple more, eventually revealing the Airstream in all her glory.

I complete several circuits of my new home before I finally come to a stop next to Tyler. "Wow, she truly is gorgeous."

"Yes, yes, she is."

Tyler's words having a distinct rumble to them. I look up at him, surprised to find he's looking at me and not the travel trailer. Color floods my face before I realize he must have looked down, as I looked up.

To help cover my confusion, I open the narrow door. Just how narrow becomes apparent when Tyler sets about manhandling my large suitcase inside.

He manages it, although by the time I've joined him with the rest of my bags, there's no room left to swing a cat. It's not lost on me that there had, until recently, been plenty of cats on hand to swing.

Next to me, Tyler is silent as he takes everything in. I'm a little gob smacked myself. If I'd thought the place looked good yesterday with most of the windows covered, now it's a sight to behold.

Light floods the space thanks to all the windows and a couple of skylights. There's no missing why Airstreams hold a special place in America's heart. The silence lengthens to the point it overwhelms me, and I blurt out the first thing that comes into my head.

"It's not much, but it's home." I'd normally follow this up by holding my arms out to the side, only there wasn't enough room. At least not without being squashed up against Tyler.

Awkward doesn't explain how I am to find myself jammed in here with a gorgeous man like this. Interestingly, he appears completely at ease, his stance relaxed, a soft smile playing on his lips.

"I've gotta say, it's a hell of an improvement on the main house." He then surprises me by opening a small panel in the wall next to the door. Inside there's a jumble of fuses and other bits and pieces. I wouldn't have a clue what they're all for, yet Tyler seems familiar with them.

"The wiring looks to be in good working order, so I'm guessing whoever owned the main house must have lived out here." Safe in the knowledge he won't risk electrocution, he flicks the light switch, with both of us surprised to find the lights work.

He turns them back off; he turns them on again. "I thought you said the utility company wasn't coming until later today."

"I did, they did." A quick look at my watch confirms it is just after ten-thirty. There wasn't a chance this would happen in the city, with it more likely they'd be days late turning up rather than early.

"Hmmm, I wonder?"

Without telling me what he's wondering about, Tyler takes a step in my direction. Even with the windows uncovered and the lights on, I'm in the dark until he reaches out and taps on the accordion door to the small bathroom.

"I'll have a quick look at the plumbing while I'm here, if that's okay with you?"

Because of the narrow confines of the Airstream, the only way he can do that is by inching past me, something I'm not sure I'm comfortable with. This doesn't mean I wouldn't like him up close and personal, but that I want to keep my attraction to him to myself.

This has me backing up to the point I trip over the end of a small rag rug in the aisle, landing on the double bed with a hard bump. I'm doing my best to right myself when Tyler breaks into a broad grin, which then escalates to booming laughter.

It's infectious with me soon joining in. Better this than wallowing around on the world's hardest bed feeling sorry for myself.

I get even when I watch Tyler attempting to enter the small bathroom. Short of some WD40 and a pry bar, I doubt it's possible. And if he were to succeed, it'd be more than likely he couldn't get out again.

With his bottom half sticking out of the small bathroom, I'm free to drool as much as I want. "Now there's a bathroom fitting I could get on board with."

I'm unaware of having said this aloud until I hear a spluttered, "Excuse me?" A second later and he's turned off the taps, and has backed into the narrow aisle all while looking at me. His eyebrow quirked.

"Oh, ah, I was just saying the bathroom fittings, ah, probably aren't, ah, up to code." As garbled as my response has been, it takes a second for his brow to clear, as he does his best to make sense of my ramblings.

Obviously deciding he must have misheard me; he runs his fingers through his hair. "It should be okay for now." He slides the accordion door shut, clipping it in place. "Before that pipe in the kitchen blew on me, I was about to head down to Tremaine

Hardware to order a few things. Do you want to come with me and check out some fixtures and fittings for the bathrooms and kitchen?"

He looks briefly at my large suitcase jammed down next to the dinette. "Unless you want to unpack first? If you do, I can wait for you."

Unpack my case in front of a man like this? Hell no. While my granny underwear might be comfortable, I don't want it seen by anyone like Tyler. He wouldn't know this change in underwear style was in response to my divorce being made final.

No longer did I have to wear the racy lingerie Mitchell preferred.

No longer did I need to lure my husband into the bedroom.

No longer did I worry about conceiving. That ship, ah crib, had sailed.

As casual as this last thought has been, there's nothing I can do to stop the hitch in my breathing and the constriction in my throat.

It therefore takes every ounce of concentration for me to say, "That's okay. I can unpack this evening."

. . .

The drive into town would have been silent, if not for the volume of the country music Tyler had insisted that we listen to. I'll be the first to admit that I'm not a fan of country music. But when I saw the joy as he sang along, there wasn't a chance I was telling him to turn it off.

It's a far cry from the jazz Mitchell is a fan of. Tyler's truck is also a far cry from Mitchell's Mercedes coupe. And yet, as we pull into the parking lot at the biggest hardware store in town, I wouldn't change a thing.

TYLER

What was I thinking when I invited Lily to come with me to the hardware store? The invitation was out before I'd thought it through, which wasn't like me at all. I've got too many responsibilities in my life to go off-script.

It was this, more than an abiding love of country music, that had me singing along to the radio. There was something about the woman that had my words coming out all wrong. She has me saying things I don't mean to, like that crack about her wanting me to keep to my boxers.

And for once in a long time, I want to make a good impression. I want to compare favorably with her ex. A man who Alice had nothing good to say about, although she was staying tight-lipped about what led to Lily's divorce.

Despite allowing me to open my truck door for her when we left her place, she's quick to exit the vehicle on her own at the hardware store. Likewise, she keeps some distance between us as we walk across the crowded parking lot towards the front of the large store.

Conscious of not wanting to wander around the store like a married couple, as soon as we're through the automatic doors, I turn to her.

"I'll be out in the lumberyard." I wave my arm wildly in that direction, coming close to taking out a staff member in a bright green apron. "Oooh, sorry. Didn't see you there."

My arms safely back down by my sides, I briefly shake my head to center my thoughts. "I can catch up with you in the kitchen/bathroom section once I've finished."

When she doesn't immediately move, I point her in the right direction. I've not taken more than half-a-dozen steps on my way to the lumberyard when I think of something. This has me retracing my steps and hurrying after her because the girl can move.

And I don't just mean how fast she's walking, with the sway of her hips mesmerizing. Thanks to this, my, "Lily!" when I call out to slow her, has a strangled quality to it. Fortunately, it's loud enough to cut through the background noise, with her stopping and turning to face me.

On joining her, I've already got my phone out. "There are some price ranges you should work with. Last thing you want is to get in so deep you end up losing money on the joint."

She nods slowly before she speaks. "I guess that makes sense." She then looks at my phone. "You can email them to me, if you like."

"Oh, yeah, okay." With nothing else to delay me, I do just that and am soon headed back the way I'd come. Well, that didn't go how I'd expected. Or was that hoped? Because now that I think back on it, part of me had wanted to join her as she looked around.

"Damn it, man. You've got work to do. How about

you get on and do that?" As loudly as I've said this to myself, a guy browsing the power tools straightens as though caught doing something he shouldn't.

Rather than explain that I'm slowly losing my mind thanks to a tempting brunette, I pretend I had said nothing and speed off. I've got lumber and other supplies to redirect to Lily's place so we can start work on Monday.

Because I'd planned everything out the night before when putting the costs together, I'm able to rush through everything. There are a few extras we'll need to order in, but nothing that will hold us up.

I then make quick work of walking the length of the store, soon spotting Lily in the middle of a large display of bathroom ware. She's next to a free-standing soaking tub I know will blow the budget.

It's not until I'm next to her I spot that, rather than be looking at the tub, she's looking longingly at what's sitting in the bottom.

She glances at me before returning to gaze at the small boy sitting in the empty tub. "His mom put him in there while she looks at tiles. I said I'd watch out for him."

There's something about the way her voice catches on this simple statement that has me looking more closely at her. However, there's nothing to show on her face as she looks across the open space to the woman dithering over tiles.

A brief look in the same direction and I know why the boy in the tub had looked familiar.

"Have you looked at anything yourself?" I hunker down next to the tub before carrying on. "I can keep an eye on this little pirate, if you like?"

Now I've got her attention.

"Oh, I'm not sure that'd be right. I said I'd look after him. I..."

"It's okay, Lily. Just let Gemma know Tyler is looking after Coby. She'll be fine with it." As if to reinforce my ability to look after the little boy, I grab the plastic sword he's abandoned in the tub next to a cardboard pirate hat.

Using my best pirate voice, I declare, "Go away with you, landlubber. Get you to yon display and select some tap ware." I follow this up by swatting Lily's ass with the flat of the blade.

By now, the small boy is laughing uproariously and doing his best to grab the sword off me. It's enough to have his mom looking in our direction, even though she's busy adjusting the sling that holds Coby's little brother tight against her back. On recognizing me, she returns my jaunty salute with one of her own.

"See, it's okay. Off you go. Check out what you think would work with the vintage look in the kitchen. We can then use the same theme in the bathrooms."

With the way she leaves my side, you'd think I'd asked her to walk the plank. Eventually, though, she wanders off, glancing back over her shoulder until she turns the corner and disappears into the next aisle.

As suddenly as she's gone, she's back again, walking in the other direction and down the aisle she's actually after. "That woman needs a treasure map, because she's lost for sure."

Just how lost I've yet to find out.

SIX

LILY

I stand before the tap ware display, tears streaming down my face, a deep sense of frustration and heartache washing over me.

Every tap on display seems to mock me with its sleek design and unattainable price tag, reminding me of all the things I'll never have. The weight of my unfulfilled dreams and desires presses down on me, threatening to crush me under its relentless force.

But then, as if by some miracle, I find a couple of tissues in my pocket and, with a haphazard swipe, slow my tears. Mitchell's patronizing comments continue to flood my mind, adding to the already overwhelming mix of emotions.

Anger and frustration bubble up, like a simmering volcano ready to erupt, leaving me struggling to regain my composure. It's this that has me staring at the very top shelf. Apparently, if you look up, it blocks your tear ducts, with mine definitely needing help in that department.

Damn it, until I'd seen Tyler hunkered down next to that young boy, I'd thought I was getting over the whole being a mom thing.

Until that happens, I'm better off on my own. And yet, part of me isn't ready to give up hope entirely. The possibility of finding love and starting a family still lingers, even with the fear of more heartache lurking in the shadows.

If I was to go into a relationship now, I'd only open myself up to yet more sorrow. Once again, I'd be back wondering if I was pregnant every time my cycle ran late. I can't put myself through that again, not this soon, maybe never.

With a final, clumsy swipe at my eyes, I take a deep breath and focus on the taps in front of me. I'm determined to find one within my budget and put the pain behind me, at least for now.

And then my gaze lands on the most spectacular kitchen faucet. It's black, with a plethora of knobs and levers. This is the sort of fixture you'd plan your entire kitchen around. It's also definitely out of my budget. I need to remind myself it's not my house I'm renovating, technically it's Nanna Dot's with her having paid for it.

For all that any of that matters in my desire for the piece. I'm tentatively reaching out to see how the various levers work when Tyler breaks my reverie.

"No, Lily, step away from the Kohler. This is not a drill! I repeat, step away from the Kohler!"

Tyler's instruction has a drill-sergeant quality to it, and I yank my hand back in response. It's only on hearing high-pitched laughter that I actually turn and look at him.

He's not alone. The little boy now sits proudly on his shoulders, holding his plastic sword aloft. However, it's Tyler who's wearing the pirate hat. Where he'd gotten that eye patch, who knew?

And just like that, my melancholy dissipates. I know it's not gone for good, only gone for now, and that's good enough for me. I need to move on. It's as I watch Tyler staggering down the aisle a la Captain Jack that an idea sparks.

On us arriving back at the house, loaded down with various tile samples and brochures of the taps and fittings I can afford, I've come to no conclusions. I've heard of other women doing the whole 'friends with benefits' thing, but I'm not sure it's for me.

There's also us effectively working together. Imagine how awful it would be if we got together, and it ended badly? Facing him every day and having my failure rubbed in my face was too awful to consider.

And I'm of this mind, right until I walk into the small mobile home, and Tyler follows me in. Ostensibly this is so he can put all the tile samples on the dinette table, but the way he looks at me, says otherwise.

Could it be I'm not alone in my attraction?

So fast does he drop the samples that it's a wonder none of the tiles break. The only thing that breaks is Tyler's reserve. Rather than leave as I've expected, he takes a step forward, with this having him hard up against me. It was to be expected in such a tight space.

He then stills, simply staring down at me, his gaze questioning. I know what he's asking, and yet I'm not brave enough to answer. Hadn't this been exactly what I was thinking about on the drive home?

Despite my internal argument, Tyler must see agreement, because he slides his arms around behind me, nudging me even closer. Oh yes, he's definitely as keen as I am, perhaps even keener.

When his lips drop to mine and I fall against him, there's no missing the rocking and rolling of the mobile home, this only adding to my loss of balance. I'm not going anywhere though, not with Tyler holding me as tightly as he is.

It's this, and a longing to let go of my past, that has me surrendering to the kiss, my lips parting under the gentle pressure of his. Much as I don't want to compare him to Mitchell, my brain goes there.

And as with every other comparison made over the past couple of months, my ex falls short. This is especially so with Tyler towering over me. Wrapped up in his arms, his lips moving confidently over mine,

I feel cosseted and cared for as never with Mitchell. As much as he'd always gone on about us being equals, that was only in certain departments, those that suited him.

As if sensing my mind isn't fully on our kiss, Tyler lifts his head. "Earth to Lily. If this isn't okay, you just have to say. I'm a big boy, I can take it."

Oh, my, is he ever? I'm not sure what it is about Tyler, that has me wanting to laugh. Not at him, but in pure joy. With him, I don't have to pretend to be someone I'm not. Mitchell wouldn't have gone near me dressed as I am now.

With Tyler, I can be myself.

I'm not sure who's the more shocked when I blurt out, "Oh, you're definitely a big boy," following this up with a distinctly unladylike snort.

His grin is soon a match for mine. "Baby, you've seen nothing yet!"

When he reaches around, grabs my ass and grinds me against his length, I'm in no doubt.

Okay, this could work. However, I want him to know where I stand, where he stands. This has me pulling back just enough that I can look him in the eye. Only once he's focused do I tell him how it'll be. "Just so long as you know, it's only casual. This, this can't go anywhere."

As much as I'm telling him, I'm also telling myself. By compartmentalizing my life, I can protect myself. Right?

TYLER

Just as it had surprised me when I'd invited Lily to accompany me to the hardware store this morning, I'm as surprised by my making a move on her now.

And does she really mean it when she says she wants to keep things casual? That's unusual for a woman. I also need to consider my gut telling me that there's nothing casual about this woman. Things could go so badly wrong, and if Ethan were to find out, there'd be hell to pay.

While he's a reasonably easy-going boss, the one rule he has is that you don't screw the client. Brad had come close to losing his job when he hooked up with Macie, and it's not a risk I should be taking.

I'd been charging myself out by the hour as a laborer when Ethan offered me the role of supervisor at

Lucky Break. It was a role that allowed me to take time off to help with Zoe when needed. It also paid a heap more than any of my other jobs to date.

Lose it and it'd have a massive impact on what I could provide for Zoe. It'd for sure put a dent in my contributions to her college fund. And yeah, I know she's only four, but I want her to have the things in life that I didn't.

I forget all this the second Lily's breasts squash against my chest. I haven't reacted to a woman like this since when Jade and I had gotten together all those years ago.

Could my body be telling me it's time to move on with my life? It's not a decision I can take likely lightly with this affecting Zoe's life as much as mine.

I have to be damned sure before I commit to anything, anyone. I don't want to introduce my daughter to a never-ending line-up of partners, as I've seen happen with other single parents.

Okay, I get it, people get lonely, but it's still tough on kids having to deal with the potential fallout of messy break-ups. I certainly don't remember mom going on any dates after dad decided he preferred being single.

As surprising is the realization, I want to introduce Lily to Zoe, already able to see them laughing together in my mind's eye.

Eventually, my body tells my mind to shut the hell up and just make the most of the moment. To take it for what it is. To forget about my responsibilities if only for five minutes.

Without taking my lips away from Lily's, I open one eye. While not huge, the bed at the end of the trailer is definitely big enough for our needs. With our destination confirmed, I move us in that direction, the trailer rocking and rolling violently.

Soon enough, the back of Lily's legs hit the edge of the bed and I carefully lower us to what proves to be a rock-hard mattress. Great, if you've got a bad back, not so good for anything else. It's just as well I have no intention of taking things too far at this stage, because that bed would leave us black and blue.

There's also the continued movement of the trailer to contend with. If we were to get hot and heavy, the damned thing would probably fall off its supports. This has me making a mental note to shore it up before we take things any further. It's also a thought that has me stopping where I am, with Lily freezing next to me.

Despite our enforced stillness, the caravan keeps moving. "You might need to look at replacing the struts and springs. It shouldn't keep moving this long." This sparks another thought, although this one is less about springs and more about movement. "It could be fun, though."

I see to the second when she gets my drift, her eyes widening in response. It's when she bites her lips that I know she's trying to stop herself from laughing.

Strange, but when I first met her, she didn't strike me as the giggly sort. Although, I'm not one to talk, having laughed more in the last day or two than I have a long time.

As my focus zeroes in on those plump lips of hers, I no longer feel like laughing. This has me swiping my thumb across her bottom lip, with her trembling in response. I want to be closer than this, but that's simply not possible with us half draped over the side of the bed.

"Let's get more comfortable." Without giving her any further instructions, I inch my way across the mattress, taking her with me. The bed feels even firmer now. It's something that has me lifting the edge of the flowery comforter, my lips parting from Lily's in surprise. "Well, that explains why it's so damned hard."

"It sure does." There's a breathy quality to Lily's voice that has me looking away from the sheet of plywood and focusing on the goddess I'm sharing it with. "Not that wood, you cheeky woman." I knock on the bed base for clarity before reclaiming her lips.

She's got the right of it though, with my cock giving the bed base a run for its money in the wood department. It wins out over the sheet of ply when one of Lily's thighs makes contact in a way that says it's been on purpose.

When she gives me a second nudge, I'm left in no doubt and break our kiss. "Sorry sweetheart, but we won't be going there today."

"We won't?" Disappointment tinges her words. However, it's the hurt in the background that I find most distressing.

This has me kissing her again, throwing every ounce of passion that I can into the kiss. She needs to know I want to, but I can't. I then kick myself mentally.

And how the hell is she supposed to pick all that up from a kiss?

It was something Jade used to give me grief about, with "I'm not a mind reader, Tyler," being a common refrain at our place.

Again, I break the kiss. "Not that I don't want to." She opens her lips, looking to question this, but I press on. "Apart from us potentially knocking the trailer off its moorings, I don't have any protection with me."

I'm not sure which of my various statements has color flooding her face, her eyes no longer alight with laughter. Her response to this is a shopping list of, "It'll be fine, I can't... I mean. My cycle... um... Yeah, it'll be okay."

Her laughter after this checklist has a forced quality to it that has me looking at her more closely. For all the good it does, with her emotions now firmly tamped down.

"Hey, I didn't say we couldn't have fun."

I emphasize this when I snake my hand under the bib of her overalls, eager to see what's hiding behind the shapeless garment.

I'm not disappointed, and neither will Lily be by the time I've finished with her.

SEVEN

LILY

To ignore the bed base digging into my ass, I focus on Tyler's hand as it cups one of my breasts. It's not enough. I want to be closer to him. So much closer.

I arch my back in silent invitation, jamming my breast against his large hand, and am met with muffled laughter. There's nothing funny about his next move, with him unbuckling the front bib of my overalls with a mere flick of his wrist.

I'm only aware he's folded it down when he stops kissing. And then it's only so he can lower his mouth and bite first one nipple, and then the other, through the lace of my bra.

Even with the temperature in the trailer being well into the eighties, his mouth is hot by comparison. Despite that, it's not enough, and I fumble with the front closing of my bra, desperate to remove this last barrier between us.

Tyler, realizing what I'm up to, takes over, swiping the lacy fabric to the sides, before he stills. Rather than keep biting my nipples, he instead stares at my breasts, desire darkening his eyes. "So beautiful."

Now I don't know which breast to focus on, although Tyler appears to be having no trouble. While he lazily rolls the nipple of one, he alternately tongues and bites the other. It's almost too much, although when he pulls back and staggers to his feet, I'm bereft.

But not for long, with him grabbing the bottom of my overalls. Soon enough, he tugs on them, with me lifting my hips clear of the bed to make their removal easier. It's then I remember my granny panties, covering my face with my hands to hide my embarrassment.

Tyler's bark of laughter is loud in the confined space. "They're sensible, I'll give them that." It's a relief when he follows this up by yanking them free and dropping them next to my overalls. I'd rather be stark-naked than have a man as hot as Tyler looking at me wearing a pair of 10-pack bargain-bin panties. Beige doesn't look good on anyone, especially someone who's also beige.

But the disrobing doesn't finish there, with Tyler ripping his t-shirt over his head and tossing it on the floor. His boots and jeans follow, leaving him back down to those satin boxers. However, that's as far as he goes, confirming he's sticking to his decision not to take things too far.

It's a decision I hope to reverse, and soon. For once in my life, I want to experience making love purely for the physical joy, and without the pressure of conceiving.

And despite Tyler effectively being a stranger, part of me knows that making love with him will be fun. I usually wouldn't move this fast, but I figure he's received the Alice and Dot stamp of approval. Despite his bad boy image, their liking him says he's a nice guy who I can trust.

It's something I probably should have noted in the past with Nanna Dot, never a fan of Mitchell, and vice versa. It didn't help that her old lady asides as to his character were all too often audible.

As Tyler kneels on the bed next to me, the trailer wobbles wildly, a movement I hope my tummy doesn't replicate. Maybe I should have gotten the liposuction Mitchell had always pushed for?

I've barely finished kicking myself for not going ahead when Tyler splays his hand across my stomach. "Damn, but I love a belly on a woman." To my mortification, he squeezes it and I freeze.

"Oh, sorry, you don't like that?"

Unsure if he's talking about my belly, or him squeezing it, I slowly shake my head in answer. For me, there's shame in admitting to someone else that you hate a part of yourself. And anyway, my throat is too tight to respond in words.

"I'll try not to squeeze it again, but I'll make no promises. It's too damn tempting." Instead of an apology, he dips his head and drops a kiss on my unloved tummy. It's when he repeats the gesture that I understand he genuinely likes it, and the grip on my throat releases.

Only after swallowing and clearing my throat am I able to speak. "Are you sure you need to leave those on?" I wave a hand wildly at his black boxers as if to clarify, even though it's unnecessary. The only other thing covering him are those gorgeous multi-colored tattoos that snake from shoulder to wrist.

"It's probably best. I know you say you can't, ah hem, that you... But, yeah, for now, I'll leave them on." He then softens his rejection, by adding, "But trust me, next time I'll be better prepared."

With the words 'next time' ricocheting around my skull, I'm taken by surprise when he runs his thumb through my cleft. My body is quick to respond, though, with my hips jerking without conscious thought.

"Like that, do you?"

In response to my jerky nod, Tyler runs his thumb across his tongue before getting back to it, slower this time, with more pressure. It's when he shuffles down the bed and splays my legs wide that my body truly comes alive.

Mitchell would never...

The moment Tyler's fiery mouth covers me, it incinerates all thoughts of my ex-husband. My entire focus is now on that one point of me being lavished with attention. Sucked, nibbled, licked, and combinations thereof, all of them driving me wild, my body tensing in readiness.

I'm on the very edge of oblivion when Tyler slides one, and then two, of his fingers deep inside me. In and out, slowly at first, and then faster and faster, with my muscles clenching against them in hopes of, of... I don't know.

Eventually, I decide I don't care. As lost as I am, I take a second to realize the keening I can hear is my own. It fills the small space as Tyler's fingers stretch me wide.

Of course, it's at this point that the struts under our end of the trailer decide they want in on the action, with them giving way in spectacular fashion. It's something that has his mouth mashed hard against my clit, and that too is okay.

It's more than okay when the rocking of the trailer in concert with his tongue swirling around my clit, and his fingers plunging in and out of me, proves too much. As much as my body surrenders, so do I, for once, forgetting about conceiving, simply feeling, experiencing and living for the moment.

Why, if it was so perfect, do I want to cry?

Tears because it was so freaking wonderful?

Or would they be tears for all the times with Mitchell when it had been more to do with timing, temperature, and hormones, than anything approaching satisfaction, or indeed, love.

Had all those years of desperately trying to conceive blinded me to how beautiful making love could truly be? While I whisper 'yes' to myself, Tyler still looks to have heard me, his brow scrunching in response.

TYLER

Lily shattering beneath my mouth like she had would be almost as good as my being buried is her slick depths. Almost being the sticking point. Usually by now, I'd be all for snuggling, but the piece of ply we're stretched out on doesn't support this.

There's also the minor issue of the struts under the trailer having given out at the exact point Lily peaked. For a start, I'd thought her shrieks were in alarm, but they'd soon morphed into drawn-out moans that were a match for my own.

Damn it, I'm so close to losing it, to forgetting everything, getting rid of my boxers and burying myself as deep as I can go. But I can't, I've got responsibilities enough, without adding to them.

Lily wouldn't be the first woman to say she was safe when she wasn't. And as much as I'd love to give Zoe the little sister she so often asks for, that's not happening just yet.

I'm careful when I stand, for all the good it does, with the trailer acting like a damned fairground ride. "It might be better if we get dressed outside." To get dressed with the trailer moving around like this would be to risk smashing into something.

If it was anything but an Airstream, this wouldn't bother me too much, but they built these things solid. It's for this reason that I bend over carefully and grab all our clothes off the floor.

"Stand up and hang on to me. It'll be safer if we get out of here as one." It's looking down at Lily spread out on the thin counterpane that brings it home to me just how attractive I find her.

As cheesy as it sounds, there's something earth goddess about Lily with her lavish curves, milky white skin and long, dark hair. She's a polar opposite of Jade in that department.

However, if you were to put her next to Zoe, they could be mistaken for mother and daughter, with Zoe taking after my side of the family.

As instructed, Lily inches her way across the bed and gets slowly to her feet, her hands all over me as she fights to keep her balance. As if joined at the hip, we slowly inch our way along the narrow aisle to the point we're above the wheels and the trailer levels out again.

I don't breathe properly until we're safely on the ground next to the trailer. Thank goodness for all the citrus trees and climbers hiding us from the neighbors. It gives me a good idea, though.

Making love to Lily on a blanket in the dappled sunlight appeals on a lot of levels, least of all being that we'd be on firm ground. Despite our general concealment, Lily is still quick to dress, even keeping her back to me.

"Damn it, woman, but you've got a fine ass!" When I follow this up by squeezing her peachy cheeks, she squawks in alarm and pulls away. "Relax, would you? No-one can see us here." I snake my hands around and rest them on her tummy, my head dropping so I can kiss her on the side of the neck.

It's a maneuver that sees me with a mouthful of silky hair. "If you head into town and grab a mattress of some sort, I can fix the struts. There's no way you can sleep in here tonight without either of those being fixed."

By the way she whirls around, I can see she hasn't thought of either of these points. "Oh, you're right. There isn't a chance I'm moving back to that motel." She's already taken a couple of steps toward her car when she stops. "But what size shall I get?"

I step over to join her, pulling her in for a tight kiss. "You wait right here. I'll be back in a second." I'm soon on my way to my truck to grab my laser measurer. Honestly, with Lily, I should always have it with me.

I make quick work of collecting it, and then measuring the space, yelling the measurements out to Lily rather than her join me in the trailer. There'll be plenty of time for that.

The size of the mattress punched into her phone, and she's ready to leave again. I'm not finished with her shopping list. Not yet. This has me pulling her in for another brief kiss. "Now, if you were to get some condoms while you're in town, we could road test the mattress when you get back."

Her face floods with color, and there's a distinct hitch in her breathing. Her words, when she stutters, "what size?" have a breathy quality to them.

In answer, I simply look down. And after Lily has done the same, she bursts out laughing. "Okay, extra small it is." She doesn't wait around for my reaction, shooting off through the trees before I've a chance.

"You'll keep!" I yell after her, before following in her footsteps, a huge grin in place. There has to be something around this dump that'll support the trailer enough to cope with everything I want to do to Lily.

This stops me in my tracks. No, that's not right. It'll need to cope with everything I want to do WITH Lily. She's definitely a 'with' kinda gal, because if she's got the nod of approval from Alice at the Rose Haven, then I need to treat her with respect.

To a degree, because as I watch her clamber into her car, my thoughts are disrespectful. No, make that disreputable.

EIGHT

LILY

It's only after I've backed out onto the road, and put the car in drive, that the enormity of what just happened, makes itself at home in my brain.

If only my brain had been engaged earlier. A glance to the side and I see the very delectable Tyler standing in the middle of the driveway watching me.

In response to his bright smile and cheery wave, I give a weak one in return. He doesn't appear to be having second thoughts, so why am I?

Could it be because I've known the guy for all of one day, and here I am on my way to buy condoms and a mattress? Yeah, that will give a woman pause. The mattress would be one thing, with me needing that anyway. But condoms?

Eyes back on the road, I drive slowly off, with a peek in the rear-view mirror enough to show Tyler is now out on the sidewalk. Another brief wave that I half-heartedly return, and he disappears up the driveway.

It's only when I'm near the middle of town that something else hits me. The chances that I'll know whoever is selling me those condoms is practically a given. My foot eases up on the accelerator, to the point I have to pull into the curb to avoid stopping in the middle of the road.

I can't just waltz into the nearest pharmacy and pick up extra-large condoms. What will people think? The mere thought of asking for 'extra-large' has me reaching out and turning the air-conditioning up, the jet of cold air welcome.

The last time I bought condoms was years ago, and that was when I was living in San Francisco, where it was easier to do so incognito. It'll be a different story buying them in Coogan's Break.

Here, the chances I'll have gone to school with the person selling me the protection are almost as high as the purchase getting back to Alice via the grapevine. I can't do it, I just can't.

It's close to four in the afternoon before I return to the house in a state of high nerves and excitement. While there's a vacuum-packed mattress jammed across the back seat of the car, there's also a selection of condoms stuffed in my purse.

It had been both a blessing and a curse when none of the local furniture stores had a suitably sized mattress. They were all either too big, too small, or innerspring, resulting in a drive to Taylor's Mistake, the nearest city of any size.

Only there was I able to find a roll-up style mattress that was close to perfect. It was also there I could safely buy condoms on the sly. It was for that reason I'd gone large with the purchase, in more ways than one.

Tyler wouldn't be the first man to have an inflated sense of his own, ah, um. I'd therefore grabbed a variety of sizes, just to be on the safe side—pardon the pun—because I'd driven far enough today.

While Tyler's truck is still out front, there's no sign of the man himself. And I'll need to find him because I can't unload that mattress on my own. Despite being a solid tube of memory foam, it weighs a ton, and it's awkward.

This sees me calling out to him at the backdoor of the house, but there's no response. This tells me he must be down at the trailer, firming up the supports like he'd promised. Again, I have to fan my face as images of why this is necessary flood my mind.

Honestly, woman, get a grip. You're an adult, he's an adult, what you're about to do isn't against the law. *No, but maybe it should be, because the effect that man had on my previously frigid body should be illegal.*

There, I've admitted it. That orgasm earlier was the first I hadn't had to fake in years. With Mitchell... I couldn't. It was quicker to moan twice, cry out, and then stiffen briefly, than have him laboring away to the point it was boring. Literally.

I'm also not proud to admit that toward the end of our marriage, I was more interested in him coming than me. More interested in what his 'Little

Mitchies', as he called them, could do for me, than the man himself.

In hindsight, it was a blessing I didn't fall pregnant, because no baby, no matter how cherished, could have saved a marriage as dead as ours had been.

On this less-than cheery thought, I make my way over to the path through to the trailer, with that the only other place Tyler can be. Even if he'd been under the house, he would have heard me calling out to him.

I hear the music before I see the set-up, with the trailer effectively blocking my view of what Tyler has been up to. What I can see is that there are now substantial piles of bricks supporting the bed-end of the trailer.

And yet they pale compared to what I spy when I walk around the end of the trailer. Tyler is there, alright. And he looks to be ready for whatever I can throw at him.

Stretched out on a blanket next to the trailer, his body is on full display, the sun kissing his sculpted form exactly as I long to. Gone are all my misgivings about taking things too fast, gone in a flash of heat and lust.

I'm about to say 'hi', when I notice how deep his breathing is. He's fast asleep.

My smile is slow to build. Almost as slow as my steps as I inch my way back around the end of the trailer. There I put my purse quietly down on the tow-hitch, before stripping off as though my clothes are on fire.

There'll be no granny panties ruining the mood this time, because while the mattress can wait, I can't. A quick rummage in my purse, and I'm ready to rejoin him.

I don't bother with tiptoeing or subterfuge on my return, because my movements hadn't wakened him earlier. This has me dropping to straddle his sleeping form, my damp core snug against his semi-hard cock.

He's barely opened his eyes when I shower him with condoms, happy in the knowledge I've got enough of the right size to hand.

I have to give Tyler credit, though. He goes from groggy with sleep to awake enough to do justice to those XL condoms, in a flash. A flash that sees him briefly mold my breasts before his large hands trail down my tummy.

On him burying his thumbs inside my curls and pressing hard, I come close to losing it. But not enough that I don't grab one of the foil packets and rip it open with my teeth.

What follows is poetry in motion with me sliding the condom on and him helping me to rise high enough that I can take his full length in one slow pump of his hips.

As my breath comes in gasps, I have to wonder if condoms come in XXL?

TYLER

Heat! Everywhere there's heat. From the sun beating down on my skin to Lily pumping up and down on my cock. Her core is hotter than the sun, leaving me in danger of being burned.

It therefore takes me by surprise when a raindrop lands on my face, and then another. I do my best to ignore them, because I'm letting a stupid sun shower interrupt Lily and I going over the edge together.

With this in mind, rather lie there letting Lily help herself. I jerk my hips, burying myself even deeper, and then again, and again. Soon enough my cock explodes in a shower of heat an equal to the sun. Lily, crying out and her womanhood rippling along my length, says I'm not alone.

However, when a cloud passes over and I open my eyes, I see it wasn't rain that had landed on my face.

"Lily, what's wrong?"

All I get in response is a vehement shake of her head as she pulls free of me.

While many men would now run for the hills rather than deal with a woman in tears, I'm not one of them. It hadn't always been this way, but being a dad to a little girl had changed all that for me.

All too often, something would bother Zoe, but she didn't have the words to tell me what it was. Only by coaxing it out of her was I able to get to the crux of the matter.

And while Lily isn't a four-year-old, it's the best I've got for understanding females. I've got nothing to lose, especially with Lily.

She's kneeling on the rug next to me, and looking to be ready to stand, when I reach out and rub my hand up and down her arm. "Come on, a problem shared is a problem halved."

Again, she shakes her head. "It's nothing. Maybe we shouldn't..."

My heart drops. For a start, I know it's not 'nothing', it never is. There's also no avoiding the 'Maybe we shouldn't...'

With things moving this quickly, I guess I can understand she might get cold feet. This has me scrambling to think how long ago it was that Alice said the divorce went through, but I come up blank.

Was it months, a year, or only weeks since it'd happened? Am I simply the rebound guy?

I'm still trying to make sense of it, when Lily clambers to her feet and hightails it around the end of the trailer. A lot of rustling and sniffling follows before she reappears, once again dressed in her baggy overalls.

Rather than stay lying on the rug as nature intended, I roll to the side and remove the condom. A moment later and I'm standing and reaching for my clothes. Rather than stay there and watch me dress, she disappears inside the now steady trailer.

A moment later, she fires the bed coverlet through the open door onto the grass. Several ugly floral curtains soon follow. Only when I know I won't get a face full of soft furnishings, do I step over to the fold-down steps. I'm waiting for her when she exits soon after.

Much as I want to pull her in for a tight hug, I resist. Instead, I rest my hands on her upper arms both to balance myself and stop her from running off.

"Lily, I get that you're probably having second thoughts, but I want you to know that's not how I usually operate. That..." I gesture at the rug still lying on the grass, "isn't my usual ah, hem..."

Only then does she stop staring at the ground and lift her chin to face me. The sadness in her eyes hits me as hard as if it was Zoe and someone had badly hurt her. This time, I don't fight the desire to pull Lily in for a tight hug.

"Whatever it is, we'll work it out, okay?" I follow this promise up with a chaste kiss on top of her head. "Unless that is you really don't want me, ah, us..." I have to suck in a good lungful of air before I can continue. "Me, I'd happily spend tonight with you wrapped tight in my arms."

Another sniffle, and she relaxes against my chest. It's enough, for now. Another kiss to the top of her head, and I ask, "Did you get a mattress?"

Rather than speak, she nods her head, with it butting against my chin. "Okay, let's grab it and set it up in the trailer. She's nice and solid now, and while you were out, I went and got a fresh propane tank."

What I don't tell her is that I've also stocked the cupboards and small fridge with a few basics. Just enough to get her started, and enough for dinner tonight.

Okay, so my thinking at the time might have been on the selfish side, but now I'm glad of it. The last thing she needs to deal with right now is heading out to a supermarket.

Sheesh, getting that damned mattress out the back of her car is a mission. "How the hell did they get it in here? With a battering ram?"

At last, I get laughter from Lily, who's on the other side of the car, pulling on the mattress as I put my full weight against it on my side. With a rush, it frees and I sprawl across the back seat.

Meanwhile, the blasted mattress has sent Lily flying.

"Hell's teeth, are you okay?"

I crawl forward, climbing over the mattress in my haste to get to where she's lying in the weeds that pass for a garden at this place. For a start, I think she's in shock, although I soon see she's laughing so hard she's having trouble breathing.

I'm still chuckling when I spot the angel that I'd tripped over earlier. Damn it, if Lily had landed a couple of inches to the left, she wouldn't be laughing, she'd probably be unconscious. Unaware of all of this, she keeps laughing.

Not that funny, was it? It's only when I lay next to her in the weeds that I think of something. Was it that her fall released the pressure that'd been building since we made love? I sure hope so because the air has been prickly ever since.

"Come on, you." I roll onto my side to look at the gorgeous woman still giggling next to me. "Let's get this damned foam battering ram over to your trailer. It'll be getting dark soon."

As sure as I am about nightfall, I'm also sure that when that happens, I won't be here to see it. I'll be home reading Zoe her bedtime story, the same as I have every night since she'd arrived home from the hospital on her own.

NINE

LILY

As Tyler and I drag the world's heaviest mattress into the clearing next to the trailer, the sight of the picnic blanket has me back in that moment. It's a relief Tyler is busy looking over his shoulder at where we're going, allowing me to hide my reaction.

It's not as easy to hide this from myself, my emotions being messed up like they are. Had our combined release been wonderful? Yes, but it had been a lot more than that to me.

It was a reminder of the wasted years with Mitchell. To the number of times when making love, I'd been so focused on conceiving that I hadn't actually enjoyed myself. That I hadn't been present.

I'd sure as hell been present with Tyler earlier. It was something that had left me raw, the very essence of who I am as a woman, exposed for all to see. I wasn't sure how this sat with me, my always being a private person.

Mind you, I hadn't been alone in focusing on conception above all else. Mitchell had been as keen, maybe even keener than me, on starting a family. However, to him it was more about legacy, and proving his virility, than it was about being a dad.

How would he have reacted if our firstborn was a girl as it had been for Tyler? I don't need to think hard, able to imagine Mitchell's disappointment without effort.

It's enough to have me dropping my end of the mattress.

While I fight another bout of tears, Tyler manhandles the rolled-up mattress through the narrow trailer door and onto the bed. If he wasn't here, it'd still be stuck in the back of my car.

To put some distance between us, I call out, "I'll go grab the other stuff from the car." Not waiting for him to reply, I hightail it out of there, concentrating both on my breathing and not tripping in the weeds.

I've collected the high-end bedding and am walking back to the trailer when I run into Tyler.

"I've unrolled the mattress. It's not very flat yet, but it should be okay in an hour or two."

I'm expecting him to grab the large plastic bag of bedding, but he instead steps to the side to allow me to continue on. A moment's surprise, and I start up again, but don't get far, when he puts his hand gently on my shoulder.

"Sorry, but I need to be somewhere. I'll..." He looks at his boots briefly before continuing. "... see you tomorrow, unless..."

Despite knowing what he's asking, I'm not sure how to answer him. Would I like to spend the night making love to him in the now stable trailer? Of course! But I probably need to get my head around how screwed up my marriage had been, even more.

Tyler must see my decision before I've made it, because he leans in and gives me a friendly peck on the cheek. "I'll catch you in the morning, bright and early. There are a few things I have to get sorted before the full crew arrives on Monday."

I've tightened my hold on my package in readiness to move on when he leans in again. His lips brush my ear, sending shivers down my spine toward...

"Lily, I understand this all came out of the blue. Well, it did for me. But don't think for a minute I've got any regrets."

He follows this up by cradling my chin with his thumb and forefinger. The kiss that follows has me dropping the bedding, my toes curling as much as the mattress in the trailer apparently is.

With my body now aflame with need, it comes as a shock when he breaks the kiss. My lips still parted in readiness. And he kisses me again. Instead of igniting the fire within me, he kisses me platonically, leaving me feeling robbed of something.

And with that, he's off toward his truck, leaving me to carry on to the trailer. This time, when I step into the grassy clearing next to it, the rug and boxes of condoms are no longer there.

The following morning, I wake before dawn as I usually would on a Friday. However, there's nothing usual about this Friday, with my eyes gritty thanks to a night spent sleeping on what amounted to a banana. Despite Tyler's assertions that it would flatten out, even now there's a distinct curve to the mattress.

Rather than stay where I am, I struggle out of bed. As well as tired, I'm sweaty thanks to every door and window being locked tight. Even with the trailer not being visible from the street, I wasn't taking any chances of someone breaking in.

I'm sticky, with the state of the sheets a testament to how much I'd tossed and turned to cool down and find a comfy spot. Thank goodness the trailer's shower works, even if the water heater apparently doesn't.

After last night, a cold shower is exactly what I need, because it wasn't just the heat and curvy mattress that meant sleep was elusive. My dreams had been as hot as the inside of the trailer, with Tyler a constant.

I've only just rinsed the last of the conditioner from my hair when there comes a loud knocking on the door of the trailer. Loud enough, I can hear it over the trickle of cool water.

It's not until I've turned off the water that I realize my only towel is in my suitcase and well out of reach. It's something that has me popping open the concertina plastic door and yelling out, "I'll be with you in a moment."

As if sensing the panic in my voice, my visitor soon responds, telling me it's Tyler, and that he's got treats. Now I'm torn. Do I grab that towel, or don't I?

With last night's dreams still buried deep in my subconscious, it's a straightforward decision. As much as I'd decided last night that my marriage had been a sham, I'd also decided that in the future, my life would be different.

It's this that has me unlocking the trailer door and simply standing there dripping wet while I wait for Tyler to open the door. At least twenty seconds pass before he calls out, "Got my hands full."

Oooh, that's a big ask. It's one thing to stand inside the trailer and strike a pose. It's another thing entirely to step forward and play the part of the instigator.

TYLER

I don't know what I was expecting when Lily opened the door, but this wasn't it.

Am I disappointed? Hell no, although I come close to dropping the coffee and pastries in my haste to join her in the trailer. Damn it, the woman is as a goddess standing there, water streaming down her body from her hair.

I'm hardly aware of slamming our breakfast down on the kitchenette, before I drag her in for a tight embrace, not caring if my clothes get wet. A brief look at the bed and I give up on that idea. She's too wet for that, and she'll be even wetter by the time I've finished with her.

It's then I spot the picnic blanket on the dinette table along with all the samples we'd brought home from the hardware store. Hah! There'll be no dining el fresco this morning.

After sliding the samples and brochures onto the banquette, I make quick work of spreading the blanket out. Soon after, Lily is lying back on the table and I'm ready to eat.

This sees me licking, sipping and even sucking on Lily's bud to the point she's reduced to a puddle. When she comes hard enough to shake the table, I add bolstering the support leg to my list of jobs around the place.

Much as we wanted it, there wasn't a chance we could fit in that shower together, with me allowing her to go first. By the time I've rinsed off, she's dressed and ready for the day and I've added fixing the hot water heater to my list.

Before heading over to the main house, we turn the mattress over and put her monster suitcase atop, hoping to get rid of the remaining curve. Despite my being a fan of curves, I don't fancy sleeping on one.

And after the fun we'd had this morning, I know I'll be back at the trailer tonight after I've read Zoe her bedtime story.

The last thing we do is to open every window in the place along with the two skylights. It was ridiculously hot in there this morning and not all of it had been down to how aroused I get whenever Lily is nearby.

It's one reason I'm making the most of the crew not being around, and in particular my boss, Ethan. Once he's on site, I'll need to cool my response to Lily or risk losing my job.

Strange, but after working with Ethan for near on a year, it'll be the first time I've put that rule to the test. And as I watch Lily carefully removing the first of the cabinet doors in the decrepit kitchen, I know it won't be easy.

Add in my now knowing what hides under those baggy overalls of hers, and they're anything but a turn off. There's also the fact they make for easy access whenever the fancy takes us, and as the day progresses, it's amazing how often this is.

Come lunchtime, and we do, twice. Come mid-afternoon and I'm hanging out for a coffee. A quick check on Lily, who's in the front parlor dealing to the drifts of cat hair with the Lucky Break, and I see she is, too.

"Okay, break time."

Thanks to the racket being kicked up by the enormous vacuum, she doesn't hear me. Rather than shout at her, I turn it off at the wall, leading to her looking at the hose and cussing it for cutting out on her again.

"It's all good. I turned it off at the wall."

She spins around, her eyes wide, one hand on her chest.

"Sorry, I didn't mean to sneak up on you. I need a break, and by the looks of you, I'm not alone."

She drops the vacuum hose before clenching and unclenching her fingers to have them working properly again. "You're not wrong. I'll go get coffee started. See you at the trailer?"

I think about it for a second. While it makes sense to have our coffee at the trailer, if we end up back there, that'll be us for the day. As appealing as that is, there are still things I need to sort out for Monday. And while I wouldn't be averse to working here over the weekend, I've got plans with Zoe.

"How about out on the front porch?"

It's a bit of a mission getting everything set up out front, but then I'm glad of it. There's a relaxed familiarity sitting next to Lily on the top step, watching the world go by.

What starts out slowly soon turns into a steady stream of kids walking home from school, mostly in groups.

Having watched several groups pass, Lily gestures with her coffee cup toward the next lot. "That's so weird."

"What is?"

"Seeing kids walking home on their own. In San Francisco, their mom would have picked them up at the school gates." She falls silent as another gaggle of kids passes by, laughing and shouting.

There's a gentle smile playing around her lips right until we see two small girls with their mom. Honestly, all three are like something out of a Sears catalog, from clothes and hair, right down to their shiny shoes.

A sideways glance at Lily shows she's longer smiling. Instead, she's got her face as good as buried in her coffee cup.

All that changes when a little boy comes into view.

Unlike the trio who've just passed, his clothes are threadbare, with the only thing holding his sneakers together, being uneven, ratty laces. Instead of a cartoon backpack, he's carrying a plastic shopping bag.

There's also no missing that he's too thin for his height. The large sores on his scrawny arms and legs are a sure sign he's not eating well. If not for my mom's ability to whip up a decent meal out of virtually nothing, my brothers and I would have looked the same.

The boy is in stark contrast to the other kids, and by the wide berth they're giving him, his clothes must smell as bad as they look. It was something I was all too familiar with.

Next to me, Lily sits frozen, her coffee cup halfway to her mouth. Eventually, she puts it down. "Oh, that's not right." It's when she leans forward as if to stand that I reach out and stop her.

"Don't. Not in front of the other kids."

Despite the brevity of my words, she sits down with a bump, before turning and staring at me. And hard as it is, I return her gaze, refusing to look down as I had so often as a kid.

It's difficult coming clean about my upbringing. It was something I thought I'd left behind, but with Lily, I'm drawn to tell her. With her, I want to hide nothing.

TEN

LILY

I thought nothing could stop me from taking off after that little boy and seeing if I could help him out. Tyler's confession shows me how wrong I was.

"Not that our mom didn't care. She did. But after our dad took off, money was tight."

Apparently tight was an understatement, with him telling me all four boys had taken to walking with eyes downcast. They had hoped to come across spare change.

"It was also a good way of avoiding the pitying looks cast in our direction."

He falls silent as a group of about ten kids pass by, singing some made-up song at the tops of their voices.

"With priorities, mom was more interested in seeing we ate and that she paid the electricity and rent on time. She'd hand-wash our one set of clothes on the weekend."

He bursts out laughing before pressing on. "Who knows what the neighbors thought of us running around naked while everything was on the line?"

His words having painted such a rich picture, and with no more kids passing by, I grab my coffee cup and stand.

"Hmmm, I don't know. I wouldn't have minded if you were my neighbor."

Before he's processed my words, I fly down the front steps and shoot around the side of the house. He catches up with me halfway through the orchard.

His coffee cup tossed into the knee-high weeds, he grabs me and swings me around before pulling me in for a tight embrace. Our kiss, rather than being sensual, is of shared laughter that warms my soul.

On breaking the kiss, he looks down at me, obviously grappling with something. I'm about to ask him what's wrong when he speaks.

"What are you up to tomorrow?"

If not for the serious light in his eye, I'd have answered with something sexy like, "You?" Instead, I simply respond with, "I've no plans at this stage."

His smile is slow to form, but when it does, it transforms his face. This is a surprise, because after the day we've spent together, why would he think I'd say no?

"Great, we'll swing by and pick you up at nine. You'd better be ready, because Zoe doesn't like to be kept waiting."

This has me swallowing deeply. He's planning on introducing me to his daughter already? While part of me is excited to meet his little girl, another part of me is nervous as all get out. What if she doesn't like me?

"Are you kidding? Of course she'll like you."

Wait, did I ask that out loud? I don't think I did?

"Hey, I've still got some work to finish at the house." He swishes his boot back and forth through the weeds before bending over and grabbing his coffee cup and handing it to me. "You want to join me, or take it easy?"

As tempting as it is to sprawl on my bed and make like a noodle, working side-by-side with this gorgeous man appeals more. "No, I'll come back with you. But no more cat hair."

It's only as he's leaving that he tells me tomorrow's outing is to the aquarium at Taylor's Mistake. That'll be fun, although I don't know what I'll wear. I'd only packed enough clothes for a week, with those more suited to sorting out the last of Nanna Dot's affairs.

I'm not sure I've got anything appropriate for a day-trip with a little girl and her dad. Even the overalls I've been as good as living in had been a snap purchase at a local charity shop. I'd thought about buying new, but decided if they were going to end up splattered in paint and who knew what else, that secondhand would do fine.

A quick look at my watch and I know that whatever I

wear, I'll need to find it in my suitcase, because it's too late to shop for anything else.

A whirlwind of unpacking later, and I've sorted my outfit for the following day. What's odd is that I don't remember packing the flowing maxi-dress, deciding I must have missed it when unpacking after Mitchell and I returned from Mexico.

If I knew then what I knew now, I'd probably have been better off staying down that way, where the cost of living was better.

Unfortunately, in unearthing the dress, I've trashed the trailer, with not a flat surface left clear, and clothes hanging from every available latch. It's more a charity shop than a home.

The only plus to having everything out is that it's allowed me to sort through everything and even put some clothes in the built-in dresser next to the bed. If I'm living here for as long as it takes to flip the house, I may as well make myself at home.

The last thing I put away is the sexy underwear I'd bought when shopping for the mattress in Taylor's Mistake. It was when buying the condoms that I decided I'd trash my beige granny monsters the moment I got home. The only difference between now and when I'd worn racy lingerie for Mitchell is that it's now MY decision to wear it.

The next morning I'm bleary-eyed. I hadn't slept well even with the mattress having flattened out. It also hadn't helped that my dreams—make those nightmares—were full of a petite blonde fairy of a girl arriving with Tyler and declaring, "She's fat. I don't like her," and variations on that theme.

I'd learned firsthand how cruel kids could be, and so I'm not confident this morning will be any different.

Despite my nerves, I'm out front early, waiting on the steps, ready for them to arrive. It's all going as expected until Tyler helps Zoe out of her booster seat in the back.

She jumps to the ground with an exuberance that's contagious and with none of the fairy-like characteristics I'd dreamed of. Nope, I can see myself at that age. Long dark hair, a little on the chubby side, but bursting with life.

And oh, my is that girl a chatterbox with her commenting on everything from the minute she hits the sidewalk until we meet at the bottom of the front steps.

Again, this is something I can relate to, even if these days I'm more reserved.

Tyler crouches down next to her, with Zoe suddenly having come across all shy. "Zoe, I'd like you to meet Lily. She's a good friend of mine."

I am? Until he'd introduced me to his daughter, I hadn't given thought to how he'd do so, more worried about whether he'd like my outfit. I can definitely cope with 'good friend'.

I take her hand solemnly in welcome before scooting down to her level. "Hello Zoe, I'm very pleased to meet you."

Although she starts by shaking my hand, she soon throws herself at me, her arms wrapped tight around my neck. "Pleased to meet you, Miss Lily. I love your dress." She pulls away briefly, before adding, "And your house. It's lovely."

I have to fight the tears that want to envelop me in response to this little bundle of joy holding me tight. As I look at Tyler over Zoe's shoulder, there's no stopping my grin. "See, I told you it was a lovely house. Your daughter even agrees with me."

He bursts out laughing. "Uh oh, you two have just met and you're already ganging up on me? I'll have to be on my best behavior today." The wink that follows says he'd rather be misbehaving.

TYLER

Zoe pulls away from Lily, her face a picture of concern. It's something Lily spots immediately.

"He's kidding, sweetheart. We're not ganging up on your daddy. We just like something that he doesn't, and that's okay."

My daughter doesn't look convinced, reaching out to take my hand as though worried she's somehow let me down. I eventually have to stand and swing her around to rid her of her worries.

"Come on, ladies. Let's go check out some fishies."

"And mermaids, you promised mermaids!" Zoe skips ahead of us as we walk down the front path to my truck.

. . .

On arrival at the aquarium, Zoe has told Lily most of what there is to know about me, my mother, and Zoe herself. My constant requests for her to sit quietly and look for whales had been a waste of breath.

Once Zoe starts, there's no shutting her up.

And yet, I'm pleased, too, because she only chats this much when she's comfortable with someone. Her hugging Lily like she had was perhaps a surprise for all of us.

When I think back on it, I can't remember seeing her hug anyone else like that. Only my mom and I. Could it be my daughter senses something about Lily that I don't?

My little girl, once freed from her car seat, bounces next to the truck, eager to get inside. "Come on, Daddy! I don't want to miss the mermaids!" This comes as no surprise, with her talking of nothing else in recent days. I also know the Little Mermaid off by heart, being forced to read the blasted story every night this week.

Lily, rather than laughing as I am, stands wide-eyed. "They've actually got mermaids?" Next thing I know, she's got the shoulder strap of her purse cross-wise over her boobs and has taken hold of Zoe's hand. "Why didn't you tell me?"

The pair look ready to make a run for it.

I'm not sure if she's asking me, or my daughter, but it's Zoe who answers with a squeal of the type designed to damage the hearing.

"EEEEEEEE, I'm so excited! Daddy says they're not real. But he'll see."

I've not defended myself when Lily again takes me by surprise.

"Are you kidding? Of course, they're real! Come on, Tyler, we need to hurry." Lily's eyes are as alight as my daughter's, the pair of them peas in a pod as they hurry toward the aquarium.

Once inside, I do my best to get my daughter to look at some of the more educational exhibits, but can't dissuade her. It's mermaids, or nothing.

And she's got an ally in Lily, who's on the look-out for signs that will point us in the right direction. Soon enough she finds what she's after, and they take off, leaving me to follow in their mermaidy wake.

I eventually find them sitting in the front row of a score of benches facing a large aquarium that's teeming with sea life. I've got to say, it's impressive, with some large fish in there. But for a rod and reel...

I've settled on the bench next to them, when Zoe squeals loud enough to have me shoving my fingers in my ears. When I see what's set her off, my hands drop to my side.

If I didn't know better, I'd think I was facing an honest-to-God mermaid. To a four-year-old, the woman in the aquarium is the real-deal. There's no sitting down for Zoe now. She jumps up, her little nose mashed against the glass, eyes locked on the mermaid, who's now swimming back and forth.

On turning to check on Lily, I can see she's equally mesmerized, although too much the adult to jam her nose against the glass. "The Little Mermaid was my favorite book when I was growing up."

She shakes her head as if to break the spell that's being cast by that brightly colored tail. Rather than swimming back and forth, the 'mermaid' is now turning lazy circles and waving at the gaggle of little girls that now line the glass.

Once again, I slam my hands over my ears as the small choir squeal in response to a flashy tail spin. "Sheesh, if they keep that up, they risk breaking the glass. Want to move to the back row? I can still watch Zoe from there."

Lily's disappointment is palpable. I think she's sad to be leaving the mermaid to her fishy business until I notice she's actually looking at Zoe and the other little girls.

The desolation in her eyes is the same as had been there when we were watching the kids traipsing home from school. Might this be the reason her marriage broke up? She wanted kids, but he didn't?

This has me thinking back to what she'd said when I'd insisted on using a condom. I'm parking it for now, because it's way too soon to talk about things like that. Hell, we haven't even been on a date yet, unless you count today?

We've not been in the back row long when Lily sighs. "I'd have loved to see something like this when I was Zoe's age, but my parents..."

She laughs briefly at the antics of another mermaid who's joined the first, before carrying on. "They didn't believe in make-believe. With them, it always had to be educational."

A quick squeeze of her hand and I lean in so she can hear me above the racket being kicked up now that two more mermaids have joined the others. "When I was little, the closest we'd have gotten to anything like this, was hunting for shellfish at the beach."

What I don't tell her is that we were foraging for dinner without the need of expensive fishing gear. "Jade and I always talked of having three or four kids, only..." I slam my mouth shut, but it's too late.

Next to me Lily freezes and when I risk a glimpse in her direction, I see her eyes are shimmering with unshed tears. "Alice told me what happened. I'm so very sorry." It's then her turn to squeeze my hand, only facing me after that.

Unsure of how much the old girl from the Rose Haven had told Lily, I deem it safer to keep quiet. And anyway, who the hell wants to rehash an awful time in their life like that? Not when you're on what amounts to a fun family outing.

Eager to move onto safer subjects, I blurt out the first thing that comes to mind. "Hey, I'd love to be a dad again, but kids are expensive. I'd rather care for them properly than..."

As I watch her eyes sheen with tears, any other words dry up. That she wants kids is obvious in so many ways, not least of all being the way she gazes at Zoe when she thinks I'm not looking. Again, I have to wonder at what went wrong with her marriage.

I'd ask, but I'm not into the touchy-feely stuff. I'm more at ease showing people I care about them by my actions. Like showing Zoe how much I love her by taking her to see a 'real-life' mermaid, when I know it's a crock.

Next to me, Lily takes a calming breath or two before rushing out. "Kids aren't on the cards for me."

Her phrasing is strange, leaving me uncertain if it's a case of won't or can't, or that she's not interested in taking on someone else's. This has me checking on Zoe to see how she's going. Why would a woman not want to take on a kid as wonderful as Zoe? Again, I'm not comfortable asking.

However, once Lily starts, she doesn't seem able to stop. Careful to keep her eyes locked on the mermaids and Zoe, she rattles through everything that was wrong with her marriage before running out of steam.

The only thing she hasn't cleared up is whether in being unable to have kids herself, she's not interested in being a mom, period. It's one thing for her to look at my daughter longingly, it's another thing entirely to take on the responsibility full-time.

Zoe breaks the awkward silence when she bounds up and jams herself between us, now a veritable expert on everything about merfolk. It would appear the mermaids are off for a special morning tea, because even mythical sea creatures need scheduled breaks.

ELEVEN

LILY

On the trip home, I keep my eyes glued to the road, still unable to believe I told Tyler about my failed marriage and why it went wrong. In doing so, I'd as good as told him there was no future for us, not when I couldn't play the part of mom, other than on paper.

My heart races as I replay the moment in my mind, with Tyler's silence deafening ever since.

Even Zoe has fallen silent now, worn out from too much excitement and junk food. In contrast to the non-stop chatter of the drive there, all that comes from the backseat is gentle snoring, with even this tugging at my heartstrings.

I can't help but feel a pang of jealousy as I think about how I would love to have a child like her. But now, I doubt I'll have that chance, and anyway, the thought of being a stepmom fills me with conflicting emotions.

Would it be a constant reminder of my own failures? Or could it be a new opportunity for happiness? I'm not sure if I'm ready to face those questions yet, and certainly not so soon after my divorce.

Perhaps my worrying about it is academic. If Tyler is like most men, my unburdening myself will have him dropping me off without another word. It'll then be all business come Monday when he turns up with the rest of the crew.

Then I have to wonder if I'd blurted out about my inability to have kids because I knew it was all too soon to even think about it. Perhaps my subconscious had the right of it? Surely, I must be out of my mind to be thinking about starting anything new when the pain of the divorce is still so fresh?

I've come to no conclusions when we arrive back at the house. Rather, I've been making plans how I'll avoid Tyler and the rest of the Lucky Break Construction team come Monday.

The mere thought of facing them fills me with dread. Unless I find somewhere else to park the trailer, I'm facing six months of excruciating awkwardness. If I can have the Airstream towed to one of the town's trailer parks, I can leave the team to complete the flip without me. I could even pick up some contract work locally to see me through financially.

Tyler has barely had time to engage the park brake when I've undone my seatbelt and am out of the truck. There's no need to say goodbye to Zoe with the little girl still fast asleep. A glimpse of her through the window has me wanting to open the door and hug her, but I resist.

My primary focus now is my desire to run away and hide inside my snug little trailer and lick my wounds. That and make lists about what I'll need to do in order to have the trailer away from here come tomorrow night.

I'm close to the orchard when Tyler catches up with me. "Wait, Lily."

While I stumble to a halt, I can't bring myself to face him. I've already faced enough humiliation thanks to my fertility, or lack thereof. I'm not putting myself through any more of that, at least not on purpose.

There's no missing Tyler's heavy sigh, and I brace myself for the inevitable, but it doesn't come. Rather, he wraps his arms around me from behind, dropping a kiss on my shoulder. "Sorry, I just need time to process everything, okay?"

I still don't fully relax, waiting for him to drop me like I'm hot and get the heck out of there. He, however, has other ideas, kissing the side of my neck, his breath coming in puffs that warm me. "Do you have any plans for tomorrow?"

This... this isn't what I've expected, leaving me unsure how to answer. If I agree to seeing him again, won't that just prolong the agony? And yet, as I stand with my back being warmed by his muscled chest, it feels so natural, so right.

Unable to speak, I answer with a jerky shake of my head, enough to let him know I'm free, even if I'm unsure about it all.

"Great. Zoe and I will pick you up at ten."

"You will?"

He turns me around and nods in confirmation. "According to Zoe, you're her new best friend and you're invited to our picnic tomorrow." He pauses before continuing. "And I want you there because I think you might be my new best friend, too."

As declarations go, it's not momentous, but it's enough. It's more than enough to have me reaching up on tiptoes and kissing him, as though my life depends on it.

———

Monday morning and I'm woken by Tyler turning up at the trailer at the break of dawn with coffee, donuts, and that sinful mouth of his.

He puts this to good use when, after gobbling his way through a donut, he gobbles his way through me. As a bit of a sugar addict, I'm not sure what claims my attention more. The jelly donut I'm sucking the middle out of, or Tyler sucking on me?

Either way, I come close to choking on the sugary treat when a climax hits me unawares. I'm not complaining though, because I can think of worse ways to go.

It's after I take a glazed donut from the box that I have a naughty thought of my own. A quick check of the diameter of the hole, and I know exactly how I'll enjoy the rest of my breakfast.

While swinging it around on my finger, my gaze drops to his cock and I arch an eyebrow. "Okay, now it's my turn!"

As delicious as the sweet treat is, I don't hurry, meaning we both enjoy it.

This leaves Tyler with only just enough time to wash away all the sugar before the team arrives at eight, as I'd stipulated in the contract. While they could start earlier, I'm conscious of wanting to stay on the good side of the neighbors I've yet to meet. Nothing fires people up more than their morning being interrupted by banging and crashing.

With Tyler off pretending he's just arriving on site, I jump in the shower, pleased that this time the water is hot. Unlike Tyler, Mitchell had been useless around the house, with us having to get someone in every time anything needed fixing.

While he was more than capable of completing a root canal and costly veneers, DIY left him floundering and angry.

As I wash away the stickiness of this morning's fun, my thoughts return to the picnic the day before. We'd started out at the northern end of the beach, but the wind meant we'd risked sand in our sandwiches.

This saw us packing up and heading for a glade deep in the forest, the wind leaving us alone as it roared through the treetops. As we lay back on the picnic blanket and watched the clouds scudding across the sky, it was as if we were still feet away from the surf.

Thanks to Zoe's ears having the listening capabilities of a spy satellite, there hadn't been a chance to discuss my revelations at the aquarium.

This had led to an unspoken truce, in which Tyler and I simply relax and enjoy each other's company. And I was okay with that, even if I knew we'd have to face my demons soon enough. Technically, we could have talked about it when Tyler arrived with breakfast, rather than...

The memories have me licking my lips, surprised to find I'd missed some powdered sugar in my haste to shower and get over to the house.

Okay, I'd been happy enough to avoid the issue this morning, too.

TYLER

It's a close-run thing, but I fake arriving at the same time as the rest of the crew. Of course, if anyone were to put their hand on the hood of my truck, they'd know it was BS. The engine is too cold for that. Unlike myself, with my cock still thrumming thanks to Lily's donut action earlier.

For all the closeness yesterday and this morning, there'd been no missing that neither of us wanted to go near her revelation at the aquarium. While she'd said right from the start that she wanted to keep things casual, only now do I see things from her point of view.

Following a divorce and the death of the woman who'd raised her, it's doubtless too soon to commit to anything else. Either event on their own would be enough to mess with someone's emotions. Back-to-back, they could seriously screw you up.

I'm out on the sidewalk when the first delivery truck rumbles to a stop, for all the notice I take. Nope, I'm still focused on my reaction when, on my leaving the trailer earlier, Lily had stressed we should act casual in front of the others.

She doesn't know about Ethan's stupid rule, so for her to suggest we pretend we barely know each other doesn't sit well with me.

Despite my playing it safe with relationships, for Zoe's sake, being cast in the role of Lily's dark and dirty little secret doesn't sit well. I'm not a rebound kinda guy, preferring to play for keeps.

I don't have time to dwell on it, when another truck pulls up right behind the first. From there it's all go with the front yard soon resembling the back lot at Tremaine Hardware.

We're damned lucky we'd had all the big stuff ordered for the Dugan job. Without that, there wasn't a chance we'd have been able to start strongly like we are. The other thing that's in our favor is that with the footprint of the house staying as it is, there's no need for permits.

I'm overseeing the last delivery when I hear feminine laughter from inside the house and my heart speeds up. I've got no idea how well I'll be able to hide my reaction to Lily's presence. Not with the other guys around. And it isn't something I've had to put to the test before now.

I guess I'm about to find out, with me taking the front steps two at a time in my haste to get inside. On seeing Lily down the length of the hallway in the kitchen, my footsteps slow. Damn, she looks good in her overalls. Not as good as she looks out of them, but a close second.

What doesn't look good is Heath and Josh Hendrick crowding her, their eyes alight, ready smiles in evidence.

How long since the green-eyed monster made itself at home in my chest?

I've not decided when Zac Thomas comes into view and casually slings his arm across Lily's shoulders. It's a maneuver that has his hand way too close to her left breast for my liking. I'm no longer seeing green, I'm seeing red.

I don't think before taking a big step forward, on my way to teach Zac he can't manhandle a client like that, especially not this one.

The irony has yet to make itself known when I encounter that gaping great hole in the middle of the hallway. Soon after, I face plant what must be the only solid floorboard in the entire house.

I'm no longer seeing red, I'm seeing stars.

Rather than try getting to my feet, I stay where I am while I carry out an assessment of how much damage I've done. Lily soon hunkers down next to me, her hands exploring me for potential damage. "Are you okay?"

I've concluded that I've only hurt my pride when the front porch creaks alarmingly.

"Well, that was stupid."

There's no missing the drawl in this pithy observation, telling me Cole Stillman has finally arrived on site. The old guy is never on time, coming and going as he pleases and not doing a hell of a lot when he is there.

And no-one on the team is brave enough to call him on it, not even Ethan. For all I know, the old guy might not even be on the payroll, just turns up whenever Zac Thomas, his nephew, is on site.

Despite being in his late forties, there's an air of menace about Cole that has us all toeing the line, although it'd come in handy in the past.

Lily, however, has no such reservations, rounding on

him and firing, "Well, don't just stand there. Help him up!" at him.

There's no missing the sucking of air through teeth coming from Zac and the Hendrick brothers as they walk gingerly down the hallway.

"Yes, Ma'am!"

Despite my still lying there in a heap, I can almost imagine Cole has followed this up by snapping to attention and saluting. Either way, the next thing I know, I'm being dragged upright. While Cole could probably have done this on his own, the other guys have stepped in to help.

It's not until I'm standing, a Kendrick brother supporting me on either side, that Lily cries out. For a second, I think she must have hurt herself, instead she's looking at my face in horror.

"What?" I'm not up to asking more than this, with staying upright being a challenge.

Rather than answer me, she turns to Cole. "Can you please carry him out to my trailer? I'll need to check to see if he needs stitches. It's too dirty in here for that."

Stitches? What the hell is she talking about? It's about now I notice something crawling down my face, but held up by brothers like I am, I can't swat it away.

It's only when it hits my mouth that I realize it is blood, not some creepy crawly.

I'm not a fan of blood. A second after this thought crosses my mind, the lights go out.

TWELVE

LILY

As I sit next to Tyler, who's tucked up in my bed, I'm still in a state of shock.

First, he'd come close to knocking himself out by falling down that stupid hole. Second, he'd driven his forehead into a nail sticking up through a floorboard.

But, most shocking of all, was when after whispering, "I don't like blood," his eyes had rolled back in his head and he'd slumped forward.

This had the old guy tossing Tyler casually over one shoulder and carrying him back here. After a whistle of appreciation, and, "Nice digs," he'd dumped Tyler unceremoniously in the middle of my bed, and left me to it.

Not for the first time do I thank my propensity to over-prepare. The first aid kit I'd retrieved from my car had proved itself well up to the challenge of cleaning Tyler's forehead.

Half-a-dozen antiseptic wipes later and I could see there was no need for stitches, with the nail having caught Tyler just above the eyebrow. This meant a lot of blood, but not a lot of physical damage. A wound closure strip and a bigger bandage over the top to keep it clean saw him almost as good as new.

"Lily, I can't stay here. I need to get back to the house. Sheesh, I still can't believe..."

Blast, I was afraid he'd be like this. Embarrassed that he'd fainted in front of me.

"It's nothing to be ashamed of. Lots of people faint." I'd seen it often enough during my years as a dental hygienist. Big powerful guys coming in, and as soon as I got near their teeth, it was all over.

I'd learned over the years that rather than panic, I should get on with it, taking advantage of their state.

Perhaps not ethical, but far quicker than waiting for a sedative to kick in.

"It's not that. You shouldn't have touched me in front of the others."

I stop tidying the blanket across his broad chest. And at that moment, I'm back at the dental surgery. I'd been busy cleaning up after a patient when Mitchell started berating me for having the audacity to kiss him on the cheek in passing.

Of course, that was toward the end when I was the only one at the practice who didn't know he was having an affair with his dental assistant.

I take my hands away from Tyler as if burned, and stumble to my feet. "I'll ah, I'm... I need to head into town for, um, something."

Not giving him time to react, I grab my purse off the hook next to the door and escape. In my favor is that with him having so recently smacked his head into hardwood floorboards, he's slower than he usually would be. I'm therefore away before he can catch up.

A quick glance in the rearview mirror is enough to see him standing in the middle of the road, unsteady on his feet. I'm close to slamming on the brakes and returning when one of the Hendrick brothers joins him.

He'll be okay. And anyway, hadn't he just said I shouldn't touch him in front of the others, like I was someone to be ashamed of? A quick swipe at my eyes allows me to see where I'm going and I hit the gas, although I soon slow again.

Where am I supposed to go? There's nothing for me back in San Francisco other than a few belongings in storage. I've been driving in circles for ten minutes when I pass the Rose Haven Retirement Home.

If Nanna Dot was still alive, I could talk everything through with her. Soon enough, my tears blind me to the point I need to pull over. Damn, but I miss her.

Even if I wasn't the best granddaughter in actually visiting, we'd often caught up on a video call. And while she's no longer around, I've got the next best thing.

The hug Alice gives me in the reception area of the rest home is enough for the floodgates to truly open. I haven't cried this hard in ages, even if I'm not sure what I'm crying about. The divorce, losing Nanna Dot, or Tyler being ashamed of me?

It's a tossup, with all of them fighting for supremacy.

"Oh Lily, you really are in the dumps, aren't you? Come on my dear, let's go to my room and have a cup of tea. That's the ticket."

Much as tea appears to be a panacea to the old and infirm, I'm all for it this morning. When I'd made my mind up to visit, I'd backtracked and picked up some caramel-topped cookies.

As a trained dental hygienist, I should know better, especially with them also banned by management because of the damage they can do to dentures. It's for this last reason that they're buried deep in my purse.

"And so he wants nothing to do with me!" This last ends on a wail that has me grabbing yet another tissue from the family-sized box that sits on the small occasional table between my and Alice's chairs.

Alice frowns. "That doesn't sound like the Tyler I know. Are you sure about that?"

Another trumpet into the sodden tissue and I toss it in the trash with all the others. While Alice might be blind to Tyler's faults, she needs to know what a rogue he is. Sure, I'd told him I wanted it to be casual, but that doesn't mean I want to be discarded like a used tissue when it suits him.

"First off, it's a visit to the aquarium with him and Zoe and that's not even in the same town! Then they invite me on a picnic at the very far end of the beach where no one is around. And when that doesn't work out, we hideout deep in the forest. Then he..."

Alice stares at me open-mouthed, the contraband cookie forgotten in her fingers. "He took you on an outing with his daughter?!"

Is that all she takes from this? Can't she see that every time I've been out with him, it's been in secret? "Yes, he did, but..."

Alice holds her hand up to stop me where I am.

"Lily, in the four or five years since his wife died, I've never heard of him taking a woman out when his daughter was in attendance. Never!"

I take comfort in her words right up to a point. "And yet we were never where anyone could see us."

After saying goodbye to Alice, I'm sitting in the car ready to leave when there's a frantic knocking on my driver's window. It's Alice. For a second, I think she's about to stuff the rest of the cookies through the now-open window to save them from being confiscated, but that isn't it.

"Sweet pea, I just remembered something. When the Lucky Break boys fixed that leak in my ceiling, I overheard them talking about something. Apparently, their boss has a strict rule about them not fraternizing with the clients. Someone called Brad nearly lost his job over it, while others weren't so lucky. Could that be what young Tyler meant when he said you shouldn't touch him?"

"I don't know. Don't you think he'd have told me if that was the case?"

It isn't until I'm driving away, my mind awhirl with possibilities, that something occurs to me. Could it have been that, being potentially concussed as he'd been, Tyler's words hadn't come out as he'd wanted?

TYLER

After watching Lily's car disappear around the corner at the end of the street, I'm pleased Josh

Hendrick is there to help me back up the path to the house. I really did a number on myself when I fell down that blasted hole.

After he'd propped me up on one side on the front porch, he'd left me to it, a bottle of water at my side.

While I can understand why I feel like crap, what I don't understand is why Lily had lit out like she had. Even with my brain doing somersaults, it'd been easy enough to see how distraught she was after I'd said she shouldn't have touched me in front of the others.

Dammit, doesn't she know that if Ethan were to get wind of our relationship that I'd be out of a job? I take another swig of water while I think about it. It takes longer than it normally would for the cogs in my brain to click into place.

"You freaking idiot!"

"Excuse me?!" Cole Stillman follows this up by kicking one of my boots. "Mind your manners."

I'm not in the mood for this right now. "Not you, me."

A brief snort and Cole says, "You'll get no argument from me on that front. But, safe to say, your secret's safe."

My secret? What the hell is he talking about? Am I usually this slow?

Next thing I know, Brad McKenna has joined Cole out on the front porch. "Dude, you might have thought you were hiding it, but damned if you weren't stripping that woman every time you looked at her."

"Yeah, you're just lucky Ethan is busy with Lindsey and the pregnancy, otherwise you'd be up to your neck in it." Cole nudges my other boot with his. "And speaking of crap, you look like it. Take a nap in that trailer of hers. I doubt she'd mind."

His laugh after this has me itching to get up and punch his lights out, with it probably just as well I'm not capable.

I'm not even capable of getting back to the trailer on my own, with Brad helping me get there without walking into one of the many trees on the way. We complete the trip in silence, with Brad only speaking when I'm once again sprawled across Lily's bed.

"We'll cover for you, but you'll need to be careful when Ethan is around."

I try to assemble my thoughts to refute that there's anything between Lily and me, but Brad talks all over me. "Sheesh, mate, don't try that BS with me. Don't forget, I'm living with one of our clients. If not for Ethan and me going way back, he'd probably have fired me for it." He falls silent for a heartbeat. "And I know how much this job means to you, with Zoe and all."

Brad leaves me to my thoughts after promising to check on me soon.

As I lie there mulling over how to proceed, I take in all the differences Lily has made to the trailer. Mostly this is down to removing the curtains, leaving the place brighter all round.

It's a far cry from my dingy studio apartment in town. Much as I'd love to live with my mom and Zoe, there simply isn't room. As it is, I only use my studio to sleep in, heading home each night after dinner with Zoe and my mom, followed by a bedtime story.

This once again has me realizing that I can't afford to risk this job, no matter how tempting I find Lily. I fall into a fitful sleep with thoughts of this morning and how she'll react to what I've got to tell her, doing their best to keep me awake.

I'm not sure how long I've been asleep when I notice movement in the trailer. Cracking one eye open, I see Lily has returned. I'm nervous about opening both eyes, not knowing what sort of response I'll get from her. If nothing else, I need to explain why it was I hadn't wanted her touching me, and that it wasn't anything personal.

"Lily about earlier. Not that I didn't want you touching me, it was..."

She puts a large Skye High Pies paper bag on the dresser next to the bed. "It's okay. I now know why it was. I promise I'll keep my hands to myself while the others are around, especially the boss."

"Thank you. If it was up to me, it'd be different, but I need this job."

She nods slowly. "Yes, Alice explained that to me. You stay here and enjoy your lunch. I'm off to work on those cabinet doors."

She's gone soon after, leaving me to reach out and see what treat she'd bought for me. I'm not used to being waited on hand and foot like this, especially by a beautiful woman like Lily. A man could get used to this.

A man could also get used to eating meatball subs as delicious as this for his lunch. It's a far cry from the hastily assembled sandwiches I usually eat on site. Today I didn't even have those, so eager had I been to join Lily for breakfast.

Any good feelings I have toward her are out the window when I finally make my way over to the house. She's flirting outrageously with all the men, including Cole. What's even more eye opening is that with Ethan having finally made it to the site, she's even flirting with him.

This stops me in my tracks, unsure if I should intrude on the banter they obviously have going. None of them are aware I'm here, meaning it would be all too easy to retrace my steps.

Sheesh, that floorboard really did a number on my equilibrium. As I watch Lily flirting with every member of the team, I'm once again jealous enough to pass for The Hulk.

I'm giving serious consideration to getting the hell out of there when Lily looks up and sees me. The glint in her eye is one I recognize immediately, my body reacting as it always does.

After bestowing a slow wink on her, I call out, "Hey boss, I'm heading home for a while. I'm not feeling so hot." Barely giving Ethan time to respond, I start for my truck. His, "Yeah, okay, take it easy. We'll see you tomorrow," makes it to me as I'm climbing into the cab.

The only thing I'm not sure of is whether Lily got my thinly veiled hint for her to follow me. While I might not be up to my best performance thanks to braining myself this morning, I'll give it my best shot.

THIRTEEN

LILY

There had been no missing the invitation in Tyler's eyes when he'd called out to his boss that he was going home to rest.

It was enough to have me abandon the sander on the cabinet door I'd been working on and hightail it over to the trailer. I'd been in such a hurry I hadn't even said goodbye to any of the others, only realizing now how odd it must have looked.

There's nothing I can do about it now because of my burning need to follow Tyler and see where this goes. All the subterfuge might even add a certain spice to our relationship, with me never having done anything like this in the past.

I've grabbed my purse and have even made it to my car when Ethan intercepts me. "Is everything okay?"

It takes every ounce of concentration for me to plaster a smile on my face. "Absolutely. I just need to head into town to grab some lunch. Didn't get any when I was out earlier."

There's no need to be a body language expert to see that he hasn't bought into my lie, but it had been the best I could come up with. It wasn't as easy as getting away with telling patients, "This won't hurt a bit," all while hiding behind a mask.

The only thing in my favor is that because I'm the client, he can hardly call me out for it. A cheery wave and I slide into the driver's seat.

Soon enough I'm out on the road, in drive and roaring off for my first 'afternoon delight' ever.

At least I think I am, because there's no sign of Tyler's truck in the direction that I saw him heading. Could it be I'd read his signals in the wrong way? The farther down the street I drive, the more dents to my confidence.

I'm now driving so slowly that the car behind is flashing its lights. Rather than speed up and potentially miss seeing where Tyler had gone, I pull over to the side.

I'm therefore surprised that rather than see an irate driver passing by giving me a hand signal of the non-motoring type, it's Tyler and he's grinning broadly.

It's something I copy when I pull in behind him. Strange, it's only now that I realize I don't know where he lives. He'd never said. This has me wondering if we're heading for the house where his mom and Zoe live.

This doesn't sit well with me at all. I'm therefore super relieved when he pulls into the parking lot of what looks like it used to be a small motel. If I cast my mind back, I think I can even remember it being such, its gaudy turquoise neon sign flashing an invitation for people to come and stay.

Even here, Tyler is playing it cool, simply getting out of his truck and walking over to the door of a unit that sits in the middle of the block. After unlocking it, he enters, leaving the door open, presumably in an invitation for me to join him.

Short of sitting in my car and waiting, I can't see anything else happening. With a fizz of excitement, I get out of my car, and after locking it, I skip across the parking lot and into the unit.

I don't get far, with Tyler pouncing on me, his lips claiming mine in a demanding kiss. My purse drops from my fingers and I wrap my arms around him, desperate to be close after this morning's emotional rollercoaster.

Eventually, we come up for air, giving me a chance to check out the place that Tyler calls home. It's basic and tends toward the dank and dark side of interior design. Breeze block walls painted light gray, coupled with vertical blinds that have been through the wars, and my heart falls.

Suddenly, the idea of some afternoon delight isn't so delightful. Only then do I note the size of the bed. The linens are crisp and white, the pillows fluffy, but this isn't all. It's enormous as befits a man of Tyler's size, making a welcome change from the confines of my bed in the trailer.

I've lost count of the number of times I've come close to clipping my head on the dresser next to the bed. Because of the tight quarters, Tyler often opened the window over the bed to stop his head from going through it when he filled me with his glorious length.

"Oooh, I've just thought of something!" I don't bother telling Tyler what it is, rather making a beeline for the only other door in the room. Sure enough, it reveals a small bathroom, although nowhere near as small as the one in my Silver Bullet. "Fantastic! I can have a shower without bashing my elbows!"

A peek out into the room shows Tyler has shut the front door and is on his way to join me, ditching his clothes along the way. "And I can join you!"

As I collapse in a heap on the bed next to Tyler, I have to marvel at just how much fun that shower had been. It would have been even more fun if we hadn't had to worry about Tyler's potential concussion.

Despite the distractions of him running large, soapy hands all over my body, I'd done my best to check if his pupils were dilated. But the light in the bathroom being what it was, it hadn't been possible.

"Tyler, I just want to check your eyes."

He looks at me in confusion, his hand pausing on its way to give me the afternoon delight I've so been looking forward to. "My eyes? Are you sure that's the bit you're most interested in?"

A slight nudge from his hip, and I'm in no doubt there's another part of him that's ready for me to explore it.

"All in good time. Just give me a minute." A quick shimmy down the bed and I grab my purse off the floor. I've got my phone in my hand before Tyler comes to his senses.

"No photos!"

Now it's my turn to be confused, shaking my head. "Um, of course not. I want to use the flashlight on my phone to see if your pupils are dilated." The briefest flash and I'm relieved to see they're reacting normally.

"You're good. I don't need to hold back." I follow this up by slamming my phone down on the battered nightstand, rolling over and straddling him.

Tyler responds to my "Show me what you've got, big boy!" with delighted laughter, with him as eager to show me what he's got as I am to see it.

It's then everything comes to a grinding halt.

Tyler's thumbs, buried deep in my curls, are doing wonderful things to my bud, when he suddenly stops. "Damn, I've just realized I don't have any condoms here."

And even though it had once been a motel, apparently there's no longer a condom dispensing machine tucked away in some dark corner.

While it warms me, he's not prepared because it shows this isn't his usual behavior. I'm also frustrated beyond belief.

TYLER

It might be down to my recently smashing my forehead into a floorboard, but it takes longer than it should for me to put things together. She'd just come out of a long-term relationship, and I haven't dated in months. The main reason I'd insisted we use protection was to avoid an unwanted pregnancy.

With Lily unable to conceive, that's no longer a worry. And I know she'd told me the truth about that as there'd be no missing the desolation in her eyes. Learning she wasn't able to have kids had obviously devastated her.

There wasn't a chance she'd use it to trap a guy into fatherhood. My mind made up; I don't allow myself to dwell on it any longer.

"You know, we don't have to."

Lily's disappointment throws me. Wasn't she the one who said we didn't need to bother? Hadn't she said there was no need? Why the sudden change of mind? Once more, I take longer than I usually would to catch up.

Sheesh, while she says I'm not suffering from concussion, I'm sure as hell not firing on all cylinders. "Not that we shouldn't, you know. No, I was thinking we could go bareback."

Much as it would be easier to spell it out that we can dispense with protection because of her infertility, I don't want to go there. That inability on her part hurts her enough as it is, without my bringing attention to it.

While her smile is slow to start, it soon widens, exactly like the petals of the flower I'm about to claim, and without a rubber getting in the way, either.

That last obstacle out of the way, Lily doesn't waste time. Soon enough, her fiery core envelopes me when she lowers herself, taking in every freaking inch I have on offer. I'm thinking it can't get any better when she re-seats herself, slamming home with a throaty moan.

And then she moves. Slowly at first, but soon gaining momentum. There isn't a chance I can lie here like a dead man, rather I jerk my hips as best I can, matching her moves.

As stunning as the sensation of her silken core swallowing me again and again, is watching her curls as they tumble over her full breasts. Now and then, a taut nipple will make an appearance, begging me to tug on it.

The thing is, I don't just want a glimpse; I want to see both perfect mounds. This has me flicking her hair to the sides, to cup her breasts and run my thumbs over those tight little nubs.

"Oh, yes, that!"

This time when she drops, Lily surges forward, her mons grinding into me, her breasts hard against my palms. It's a move she keeps repeating until I can't hold back any longer.

The next time she drops, my cock explodes, filling her with my seed and me with the longing to be a dad again. This is as much a surprise to me as Lily's orgasm hitting a second later, her rippling muscles milking my length and emptying me to the last drop.

A moment later, she collapses on my chest, and my arms automatically wrap around her. I never want to let her go, even if that means Zoe is the only child I ever have.

Some things are more precious than procreation, and Lily is definitely one of those. It's a thought that has me tightening my hold further, glorying in our shared heartbeat.

At peace for the first time since I lost Jade, I fall asleep, content to leave Lily right where she is. Where she belongs.

———

As the days' progress, either Lily or I will find an excuse to head into town, although never right behind each other. While this doesn't happen as often as we'd like, we make up for it over breakfast each weekday morning.

The only thing that niggles me is that she's still treating it as something casual. We're close, but it's always as if there's a barrier in the way of us getting closer still.

Maybe Lily has the right of it? With us technically not a *thing* because of Ethan's stupid rule, we have to be careful not to go public. I can't afford to lose this job, not with Zoe about to start school, and the expenses that will entail.

The one thing helping us is the guys covering for me when Ethan is around. According to them, now that I have Lily in my life, I'm no longer a miserable bastard. It's something that has me less of a dictator on site, although the work still gets done.

Now I'm just as likely to be found laughing with the guys as I am to be yelling at them to stop kidding about and get back to work. The other thing that's progressing beautifully is the flip.

Despite my thinking the place was a dump, aired out and, with the rotten boards replaced, the old girl is shining. Lily had the right of it. The house has good bones.

And yet there's something missing from my life. Despite my agreeing to Lily's request that we keep things casual, I'm thinking I'm just wasting my time. If I keep it up, I risk being hurt as much as Zoe, who cares for Lily, as I do.

I won't have my daughter's emotions played with like that. My mom being the only mother figure she's ever known, I'll not upset that for any selfish needs of my own.

FOURTEEN

LILY

The morning starts like any other Friday since moving into the trailer. A gentle knock on the door and Tyler enters bearing sweet treats and much needed coffee.

While I consider myself a morning person, five o'clock isn't morning in my world. I need that coffee, although I might need Tyler first?

It's as well he's the best at waking me, at having my body on fire for the day, and for him. I'd been relieved when he'd finally accepted my way of thinking that we continue to keep things casual.

Better this when I've still to receive my final payout from Mitchell. And not so soon after losing Nanna Dot. Despite craving some sense of stability in my life, that's not to be. Not yet anyway. Maybe when I've finished the house and sold it?

Only then will I know where I stand financially. Only then will I have the head space to devote to a relationship. There's also the minor issue of Tyler letting slip at the aquarium that he'd like another kid.

And, sadly, I can't help him there.

Tyler puts the bakery bags and go-cups on the kitchenette counter. "I hope you're hungry, sweetheart." After this, he's a blur, his clothes flying in all directions. I love that he's so in touch with his body. That despite being in a hurry to strip, his movements are graceful for such a large guy.

He's stretched out next to me before he speaks again. "What are you up to on Sunday?"

One hand already snaking down my body, it takes every ounce of concentration to answer. "Nothing at this stage." This is unusual with him, often devoting an entire weekend to Zoe and her needs. We have seen little of each other at weekends since the ill-fated, albeit fun, trip to the aquarium.

"It's Zoe's birthday, so I was thinking we could head out for ice cream in the afternoon or something."

How on earth can he speak and do those incredible things to me at the same time? I'm definitely having trouble multi-tasking, my focus torn between the tension that's building in my core and considering his invitation.

In the end, I put my hand atop his, stopping him from moving it for a second. "Hang on a second. She's turning five, isn't she?"

"She sure is. According to her, she's a big girl now."

"But isn't she going to have a party?" The idea of a little girl turning five and not having a birthday party seems so incredibly sad.

Next to me, Tyler flops onto his back. "Kinda hard when she's got no friends." He blows out before pressing on, his words tinged with sadness. "She spends every day with my mom, or me. She's never been to daycare or the like."

Tyler doesn't need to add anything further. It was common knowledge, even if you weren't a parent, that those places were expensive. Him covering the costs on his own meant it had to be out of his budget.

I'm now no longer thinking about the mind-blowing sex I was about to have. I've got a party to plan. "You have her over here at midday on Sunday. That girl will have the best party a five-year-old ever did!"

Despite my wanting to spring out of bed and start making lists, Tyler convinces me it can wait at least an hour. Five minutes later and I see he's got the right of it, the tension once again climbing in my body.

A mere fifteen minutes later, and a climax cuts straight through me, every nerve ending screaming as loudly as I am. Thank goodness the trailer as well away from any of the neighbors otherwise they'd probably think I was dying here, and I am.

Sex and breakfast over, I send Tyler packing. He's gone early enough he can head back to his place in town for a proper shower. One where he won't end up bashing his elbows into the walls. He's barely left when I'm in my teeny tiny shower, washing myself from head to toe.

I've got one-and-a-half days to put together a pink-themed mermaid party for Zoe. A quick check of the weekend weather on my phone shows no rain in the forecast, meaning we can have the party in the clearing next to the trailer.

In recent years, I'd given up on the hope of ever organizing a party for a little girl. It doesn't matter that Zoe isn't my child. I'm throwing myself into this, because who knew when I'd get the chance again?

The next day and I'm up earlier than I would normally be on a Saturday, with me usually making the most of being able to have a sleep in. This sees me down in town armed with my list of party must-haves minutes after the shops open.

Pink will definitely be the dominant color, with me knowing from the few times I've been out with Tyler's daughter that it's her favorite. It was recalling her reaction to the mermaids that gave me the overall theme for her party.

As well as a starfish pinata, I get pink bunting, balloons, and streamers. On heading back to the trailer, I've even found a large inflatable 5. It's not pink, but I'm sure the silver will work just as well.

I take all of Sunday morning to set everything up, the clearing next to the trailer a veritable sea of pink by the time I'm done. With streamers, bunting, and balloons hanging from the trees, and the large inflatable 5 tied to a window latch on the Airstream, it's perfect.

Laid out on the grass are several picnic blankets with plastic cups and plates at the ready. However, the highlight of the party is the large birthday cake in pride of place in the middle of the blankets, with a mermaid sitting atop.

Zoe's reaction when she enters the space has every hour that I'd spent on the party worth it. The little girl's face is alight with joy as she takes everything in, especially that mermaid on the top of her birthday cake.

However, when I hand over a gaily wrapped present, the cake may as well be a loaf of white bread. This is especially so after the little girl rips open the present and finds the stretchy knit mermaid tail.

As I help her don this small piece of artifice, tears prickle my eyes. All my life I've imagined a time like this with a little girl of my own. It's not fair there are women out there who are mothers purely by accident, who complain of it cramping their lifestyle. Meanwhile, I'd give anything to be a mom.

Tyler is busy inside the trailer, sorting out some cold drinks for us, when Zoe snuggles up to me. "Thank you so much for my tail, Lily. I love it so much!" She then wraps her little arms tight around my waist and it's all I can do not to burst into tears.

However, her next words have my heart stuttering in my chest, my whole being frozen.

"I asked daddy for little sister, but he said they were too expensive. He said it would have to be our little secret and that I shouldn't tell anyone. But you're my friend, so... He gave me sneakers instead."

Despite these being a practical gift, there's no missing the disappointment in Zoe's voice that she's not getting the little sister she wants.

It's a feeling I know too well, having begged my parents for a baby sister for years before she arrived. To then have her, and my parents, taken from me, had devastated me, with it taking all of Nanna Dot's love to help me recover from the loss. There isn't a chance I want Zoe to miss out on a love like that, not if I can help it.

Not if I have to sacrifice what I want to make it so.

TYLER

After jumping to the ground next to the trailer, I reach back inside and grab the root beer floats off the kitchenette counter. There wasn't a chance I could risk the steps holding three glasses, not without spilling something.

I'm right next to Lily and Zoe, before I pick up that something is very wrong. Much as people talked of being able to cut the atmosphere with a knife, I'd never experienced it first-hand. While my daughter looks cagey, Lily appears distressed, her eyes brimming with unshed tears.

One thing I can't do is find out what's wrong while standing holding our drinks. This has me carefully crouching down and putting them on the tray in the middle of the picnic blankets.

After sitting on the rug next to Lily, I run my hand down her arm, with her looking like she needs comforting more than my daughter. "What's wrong?"

Rather than answer, she waves her hands around before swallowing deeply. Even if I hadn't spotted the tear rolling down her cheek, I'd have known she was lying.

This has me turning toward my daughter. "What happened?"

If I thought my daughter looked cagey before, now she's looking downright guilty. And yet I'm at a loss to know what could have happened that would upset Lily as much as she obviously is.

"Tyler, it's nothing. I've just got a headache, is all. We've been having a lovely time."

Taken at face value, Lily's words go some way to explaining why she's out of sorts, and yet I know this isn't all of it. She'd been fine when I went into the trailer to fix our drinks.

But short of giving my girlfriend and daughter the third-degree, I'm not finding out. Zoe, in particular, now has a mutinous expression that I've come up against in the past. Unsuccessfully.

I'm still staring at my daughter when Lily's hand comes to rest on my arm. "Tyler, is it okay if we call it a day?" Another deep breath and she adds, "I just want to take some painkillers and go to bed."

My take on this is don't bother coming back after you've read Zoe her bedtime story. Much as I want to rail against this, I can't. Not without upsetting both of them. Whatever happened, I'll find out, eventually. However, now is not the time.

I need to give both the girls in my life some time to cool off first. This hits me harder than I'd have expected, and I grab my glass and toss the contents into the long grass at the edge of the clearing.

Soon enough I see that neither Lily nor Zoe are interested in their drinks, so I repeat the process, hoping it doesn't attract ants.

"We'll help you clean up, and then we'll be on our way." I follow this up by stacking the tray with everything I can lay my hands on.

And just like that, it's as if the spell cast over us has lifted. After jumping to her feet more easily than someone with a headache has any right, Lily reaches down and collects the cake. Soon enough, this is back in the bakery box, ready for Zoe to take it home.

There's no missing the guilt on my daughter's face when she asks Lily if she'd like a piece for later.

"That's okay, sweetheart, but I probably shouldn't. Not with my headache."

With everything packed away and Zoe buckled in her car seat, there's nothing to keep me here. After shutting the truck door, I turn to Lily before reaching out for a kiss goodbye, but she steps back. Although it goes against every fiber of my being, I let her retreat. "I'll come by and check on you later."

Something upset her, and I doubt I'm the cause, because I wasn't even there. There's also nothing my daughter could blurt out that would have Lily rejecting me like this.

"No... No, that's okay. Once I take those painkillers, I'll be out like a light." Her words are lackluster and full of pain, although not the sort caused by a migraine, or whatever this is supposed to be.

Not giving her time to escape, I step forward and give her a peck on the cheek. "Call me if you need anything. Otherwise, I'll see you tomorrow." A quick squeeze, and I back away, giving her the space that she so obviously needs.

On arriving at the house on Monday, I'm none the wiser about what had upset Lily. Zoe had shut down when I tried asking her what they'd talked about while I was in the trailer. And when I'd pushed it, she'd had a major meltdown, to the point my mom told me to leave it.

On pulling into the driveway, I immediately see that Lily's car isn't there, which is strange given it just after five o'clock. It's after knocking on the trailer door that I know it's not just her car that's missing.

Where on earth could she be this early? Could it be she really had been suffering from a headache yesterday? That it was something serious.

I've moved onto strokes and brain tumors before I think to pull my phone out and call her. When it goes to voicemail, I'm not prepared, with my message being all too brief. This has me ringing back and leaving another.

"Lily, are you okay? I'm at the trailer, but you're not. Can you please call me? I'm worried about you."

She doesn't. Instead, I get a text soon after saying she's sorry she missed my call, but that she'll get back to me later. So impersonal is the message that it's as though she's chosen it from one pre-programmed into her phone.

It's with a heavy heart I walk down the path at the side of the house and around to sit on the front steps.

While I drink the two coffees and stuff myself with bakery items, I try to fathom what the hell had gone wrong.

And was it my fault? Then I completely beat myself up for letting Lily get close to Zoe. It was something I'd strived hard to avoid over the years, if only to protect my daughter. Strange then, that I'm now the one who's hurting.

I come close to choking on the last mouthful of donut when I think about how Zoe will take the news that Lily and I aren't 'friends' anymore.

Probably about the same as how I'm taking it.

FIFTEEN

LILY

I'm woken on Monday morning by my phone vibrating next to my hip. Initially, I'm confused about where I am, and why my body hurts so much. Soon enough the memories of yesterday and how I'd left it with Tyler swamp me.

These have me levering the recliner in Alice's room at the Rose Haven into an upright position. It's a maneuver that sees her snuffling awake, her myopic gaze soon landing on me.

As I retrieve my phone from where it'd fallen down the side of the seat cushion, I'm having trouble coming to terms with my spending the night here.

While my being away from the trailer had started out because I didn't want to be there if Tyler returned, this soon changed.

Hours spent walking up and down the beach had done nothing to make things any clearer for me. While I feel bad about how things ended between us, I can't tell him why we need to end it. Not without getting a little girl I love to bits in trouble.

But my being in love with Tyler no longer matters. I can't stand in the way of Zoe and her dream of having a baby sister. Losing my sister had hurt so much. I won't put another little girl through that. I also can't lose sight of the fact he'd said he wanted more kids.

Sadly, this is something I can't help either of them with.

As the afternoon had worn on, I'd still stayed away from the trailer, wanting to avoid the sweet memories it held of Tyler. I'd also needed some sound advice on where I go to from there.

It was for this reason I'd called in to see Alice. While the old girl could be an interfering busy-body, she also had a lifetime of commonsense to call on. It was something I appeared to be lacking of late.

As surprised as I am to wake in the recliner in Alice's room, so it would appear is Alice. Only now do I remember she'd fallen asleep before I did. While she rummages around on the bedside table for her glasses, I have a quick look at my phone. Two missed calls, both from Tyler.

I can't deal with him right now, not with my emotions still in a tangle. Far better to fire off a text message to delay what will be a horrible talk. While the chicken in me wants to gaslight him and pretend none of it happened, I can't do that.

Of course, I'll eventually have to tell him the full story of why we need to call it a day. And I'm dreading that because I know it'll get Zoe in trouble for something she can't help. My non-committal text sent I dump my phone in my purse where it will be easier to ignore.

That done, I look up to find Alice staring at me, her large owl-like glasses now in place. "That was him, wasn't it?"

I nod, but go no further.

"I hope to heck you've seen sense and told him you'll see him soon."

This has me shaking my head. "I can't, you know that."

A heartfelt harrumph and she throws the covers to one side with a verve that defies her advanced years. My having spent the night in the recliner, I'm feeling ancient by comparison.

"I want you in that shower, and tidied up, Missy!" She follows this up by pointing imperiously at the door to the attached bath.

While I follow her bidding, my heart isn't in it, although I enjoy the water pressure. I'm toweling off when Alice opens the door a crack and tosses what appears to be a new pair of underpants through the gap. The only plus in their favor is that they're not beige.

On walking back into her room, I'm greeted by a fresh pot of coffee and the rest of the chewy cookies I'd brought with me the other day. This has me thinking of breakfast over the past couple of weeks, my eyes soon brimming with tears.

I've barely sat down when Alice starts in on me. "Right, you had your turn to talk last night. Now it's my turn!"

There's a steel edge to her voice that tells me I'm about to hear a few home truths, or tough love, or whatever. There'll be nothing fluffy about what Alice has to tell me.

I don't get to say another word until she's said her piece. Her words being as shocking as they are, I couldn't have spoken if I'd tried. She falls quiet, leaving me to sit open-mouthed. My reality shoved off kilter as I couldn't have imagined.

"They adopted me!? Are you sure about that?"

"I am, sweet child. Dot told me all about it. She'd tried telling you after you went to live with her, but grieving as you'd been, it was simply too hard. After a while, it became impossible. At least for her."

She falls silent for a beat before continuing. "I told her you had a right to know, but she'd said with you truly an orphan, there seemed little point."

I take a moment to identify the emotion I'm experiencing, eventually realizing I'm angrier than I've ever been. "You mean to tell me I've spent years grieving for people who lied to me?!"

I know this sentiment makes little sense, but neither does hearing you were adopted as a baby.

Alice's anger at my words is immediate, with her slamming the coffeepot down on the table. "How dare you speak about your family like that?! They loved you, especially Dot. According to her, your mom loved you to pieces right from day one!"

She glares at me before continuing. "Family is about a lot more than blood, young lady. And from the way you talk of Zoe and Tyler, I think you know that!"

The ferocity of her words, have me pressed back in my chair, courtesy of the first scolding I've received since I was a little kid.

"You need to get past having a baby of your own. I know it hurts to hear that, but you need to consider kids like Zoe who don't have a mom."

I stare at her, unable to believe what she's just said. "What the hell does that have to do with me!? She wants a baby sister, not a mom. I can't help her with that."

My words break on the last few words, my tears yet again taking hold. This stops me from saying anything further. Alice, however, hasn't finished her piece.

"For goodness' sake. Have you ever considered she'd love a mom more? That in asking for a little sister, she'd already picked you out as the baby's mom?"

I'm still reeling from the possibility of this, when Alice adds, "And have you ever thought that Tyler would rather you over more kids?"

TYLER

Lily turns up at the house just after lunch. I don't know where she's been other than not here. There's no missing the way she scuttles down the drive toward the trailer, her eyes glued to the paving.

My being in the side bedroom means I can watch her without her being aware. Even though we haven't officially broken up, I'm hurting enough for it to be fact. That text she'd sent this morning told me far more than she ever could.

After eating both our breakfasts while sitting on the front porch, I'd called into my mom's house to have breakfast with Zoe. It was then I'd broken the news to my daughter that Lily didn't want to be friends with us anymore.

There seemed little point in delaying the inevitable, although it felt cruel letting her know the day after her birthday. And, as expected, Zoe had been distraught. Far more upset than I would have expected, given she and Lily had only met a handful of times.

Damn it, what was it I'd always said to myself? That's right, don't get Zoe involved too soon. Even Lily had said she wanted to keep things casual, and I'd ignored her, my heart overruling my head.

I hadn't been alone on that either, with Zoe wanting to spend more time with Lily following our trip to the aquarium. After that, Zoe begged me to take her to see Lily, and I'd given in because she'd never acted like this before. More often than not, she held back where strangers were concerned.

With Lily, it had been the complete opposite. From the moment the pair bonded over their love of mermaids, there wasn't a chance I could deny my daughter. That's what makes it so strange that everything had blown up at the birthday party, with the theme and the color being perfect.

When I'd walked into the clearing with Zoe, her breathing had hitched briefly before she squealed with joy, dancing around and exclaiming over every little detail. This morning had been a stark contrast, with tears streaming down her face and her throwing herself into my arms, seeking comfort.

This time, though, I can't make it better. My plan now is to pretend like Lily and I never happened and concentrate on helping Zoe to do the same. It won't be easy though because I honestly thought me and Lily had something special.

She had no right to mess things up like she did, to hurt my daughter as she had. Zoe doesn't remember her mom, with my mom, taking on the role. Part of me worries what it'll be like when she starts school and doesn't have an actual mom on hand when the need arises.

While my mom will gladly accompany her, it won't be the same, with Zoe sure to be asked by the other kids why her mom is so old. Not that I'd have expected Lily to volunteer. Rather, it was because Zoe needed every ounce of stability she can get.

The only plus to this morning is that I'm working on demolishing the old bathroom, my current mood perfect for smashing stuff. It's my fury as I go about it that has me close to braining Ethan with my sledgehammer.

If not for him stepping back as smartly as he had, we'd be on our way to the emergency room by now. Even with my having missed his forehead, he still gives me a filthy look.

"Careful, Tyler! We don't need any more accidents on site."

I prop the sledgehammer against the wall, preparing myself for a further dressing down, but it doesn't come. There's no missing Ethan's worry and I doubt this is anything to do with my nearly knocking him out.

"What's up?"

Ethan nudges some of the broken tile with the toe of his boot, all while scratching the back of his head.

"You know that saying about it never rains, but it pours?"

I nod in return, all too well aware of exactly how it goes, even in love.

"Yeah, well, you know the Sanderson place we quoted on months ago?"

Again, all I do is nod, knowing he'll tell me, anyway.

"They just said yes and they want us to move on it as soon as we can."

It's news that has me whistling through my teeth. We'd fought hard for that job, with it worth a lot of money. We can't turn it down, that's for sure, not without the word getting out that we can't cope with demand.

"I'm off down to the veterans' center to see if I can pick up some extra labor. Even if they only help with demo, it will mean we can get started." He pauses briefly while taking in the state of the main bathroom. "If you want to manage this job, I'll run the Sanderson job. That work for you?"

I don't allow myself to overthink it. Hell, I don't think about it at all. "How about I take on the Sanderson place and you look after this one?" He's surprised by my offer, and it shows. To help sell the concept, I hit where I know it will work best. "If you put Cole in charge of the day-to-day running of this job, it'll make it easier for you to get away to help Lindsey."

Even though I don't have a clue if Cole is on the payroll, the guy sure is good at bossing people around. He'll be a natural. And with him in charge, I can leave the site without being eaten up by guilt that the job will fall over. Much as Lily and I are history, I don't wish her ill.

As quick as my offer to move to the other site, is Ethan's agreement to it. He even looks to be relieved. This has me wondering if that wasn't his plan from the start. "Great, I'll let the team know what's happening. Then I'll head on down to the veterans' center if you like?"

With Ethan and I having done so together in the past, I know the sort of guys he'll be after. It's usually those who need a lucky break more than most.

Hadn't he done just that for me?

On loading my tools into the back of my truck, I'm experiencing an interesting mix of relief and regret. I'd been so sure that Lily and I had something special together, but I guess I was wrong.

Fully packed up and ready to get going, I lock my truck. Only then do I head back up the driveway to say goodbye.

SIXTEEN

LILY

I'm hiding out in my trailer, doing my best to read a book, although I'm not being very successful, having read the same paragraph four times. Despite my lack of attention, I'm still startled when there's a loud knock on the trailer door.

I freeze and my book drops to my side. I'm unsure how to tackle what will be a tough conversation. The only thing that's guaranteed is that I can't lay here hiding. Tyler will know that I'm in here.

Rather than call out 'come in' as I usually would, I get up, make my way down the narrow aisle, and slowly open the door. Only it's not Tyler, it's Ethan.

"Oh, hi Ethan."

Even after so brief a greeting, I can't help but compare him to Tyler. While both men are good looking, with a hard edge to them, Ethan does nothing for me.

"Hey there. I just wanted to see if you'd decided on the tiles for the main bathroom. We'll be starting on that in a day or two, so we'll need to order everything in."

I don't immediately answer him, knowing why it's him asking and not Tyler. While part of me is relieved, disappointment still makes itself at home. So that's how it's going to be, is it? Tyler's simply going to ignore me.

This has me looking at the tiles on the banquette where they'd landed after Tyler cleared the table in his haste to take me to heaven. Busy as I've been with him and everything since, I'd given no thought to my preferences.

However, rather than keep Ethan waiting, I turn to the banquette, grab the closest samples to hand, and thrust them at him.

"These should work."

If he's surprised by my lackluster response to this design choice, he keeps it to himself. Rather, he takes everything from me and heads back to the house, leaving me to wonder where Tyler is.

As I look at the remaining samples on the banquette, I can't help but remember the day Tyler and I had selected them at the hardware store. This has me remembering that little boy in his bathtub pirate ship.

And his mom with her baby strapped to her back in one of those sling contraptions. The sling, being blue, hinted at the baby being another boy. Give it a couple more years and those two boys would play pirates together.

Exactly as is right with siblings. Hadn't I played dollies with my little sister often enough to know how special that was? Make that adoptive-sister, with me clearly able to remember sitting with my hand on my mom's baby bump.

The first time I'd felt Rose kick, I'd been awestruck, counting down the minutes until I could hold my baby sister. Even knowing what I know now, I can't remember a single time that my parents treated Rose any differently than me.

Putting my being adopted to one side, we were sisters through-and-through.

Maybe Alice was right and my parents had loved me as much as Nanna Dot said when the pair were chatting over their many cups of tea? This has me thinking back to how it felt to have Zoe snuggled up next to me on the picnic blanket at her birthday.

We'd bonded so quickly, despite only being together half-a-dozen times. Would it matter that she wasn't my blood? I only need to think about it for a heartbeat. No, of course it wouldn't. Not having a mom wasn't a choice she'd made, just as not being able to have a baby of my own was mine.

Alice's words this morning fill my head as remorse fills my heart. "Oh, what have I done?" As mired as I am over this question, I'm in the clearing next to the trailer without conscious thought.

However, I don't get any farther, because I'm not sure what I need to do to make things right. I can't exactly walk up to Tyler and tell him I've changed my mind, and I'd like to get married and be a step mom to Zoe.

It's a little tricky saying YES, when he hasn't actually asked me. I might also set myself up for a double rejection with neither Zoe nor him, wanting me in their lives as a permanent feature.

Still in turmoil, thanks to the adoption bombshell, I'm not strong enough emotionally to cope with their rejection. And definitely not so soon after Mitchell had found me wanting and officially replaced me with a younger model.

Surely, there has to be an interim step I can take? I'm just not sure what it is. It's when I walk over to the house, after stalling for a couple more hours, that I realize just how hard it'll be.

It's then I hear Tyler is no longer on site, having moved onto another project for the company. And there's no missing the censure in the looks I receive from everyone other than Ethan.

It's not until the following morning that it's brought home just what I've lost. No light taps on the door to wake me, no sweet pastries and hot coffee, and no hot delivery man. That isn't what I miss most, though. That'd be the cuddles as we talked about the day ahead, about what Zoe had been up to, and life. I'd loved those times.

In the days that follow, everything I do and everywhere I go, I see reminders of both Tyler and Zoe. It was only yesterday that I'd gotten around to taking down the balloons and streamers from the trees.

My plan had been to give them to Zoe, but that obviously wasn't happening. Likewise, the large inflatable 5 is slowly losing air, something that should have happened in Zoe's bedroom, not in the clearing.

The other thing that's missing in the trailer is any breakfast foods, with Tyler taking care of these. After a couple of days of surviving on black coffee, I decide to remedy this.

There's only one place open this early, and that's Skye High Pies with their coffee and pastries the best on offer. Okay, and it's also where Tyler bought all those breakfasts we'd enjoyed together.

TYLER

To a background of my mom bustling about making me some of the best dang pancakes in the world, I watch as Zoe drowns hers in maple syrup. It's getting to the point her breakfast is going to be more like soup, forcing me to reach out and take the squeeze bottle off her.

"That's enough. We don't want you being sick at school."

I'm still having trouble believing my little girl has started school. Watching her leave with my mom that first day, her backpack weighing her down, had me right back with Lily. The pair of us sitting on the front steps of the house watching all those kids traipse past.

There'd been no plastic carry bag for my daughter, with her sporting what she assured me was the best backpack ever. Pink, of course, and featuring mermaids. I'm imagining what Lily would think of it when mom puts a plate piled high with pancakes in front of me. She follows this up by patting my shoulder. It's therefore no surprise, when on taking her seat opposite me, she lifts an eyebrow.

It's an interrogation technique I know all too well, and I'm not biting.

A brief huff of annoyance and mom glances to check Zoe is concentrating on her breakfast. Her hands clasped on the table in front of her, my mom leans forward and eyeballs me. "Are you going to tell me what happened?"

To give myself time to come up with something she might actually believe, I pick up my mug and hide behind it, exactly as Lily had that day. Mom's not taken in for a second, which shouldn't surprise me.

The woman is all too familiar with my various moods, often able to spot there's a problem before I can myself. It's a damned shame she can't help me this time.

I take my time finishing my coffee, before putting my mug back down dead center on one of the large daisies that adorn the table cloth. "Nothing. It's nothing." I follow this up by tipping my head in Zoe's direction.

I don't want to discuss my breakup with Lily in front of my daughter. Not with her ears now working overtime. While she might look like she's away with the fairies half the time, she's a smart kid.

Although not so smart that I can't tell she's listening in, simply by how slowly she's eating. She always devours my mom's pancakes as though afraid they'll disappear before she can finish.

Usually I'd be the same, but this morning I've no appetite.

On my pushing my plate away, mom's eyes cloud with worry. "Now I know something is wrong."

Again, I look at Zoe in an unspoken request to bury it until later, although I don't leave it to fate. Every chance she got, Zoe asked me about Lily, and while I've fobbed her off, it hasn't been easy. Even now, two weeks after the breakup, the questions are still coming thick and fast. My daughter appears as obsessed with Lily as she is with mermaids.

She'll get over it, in the same way she does everything else that takes her fancy. Better for both of us if I scrub all traces of Lily from our lives. She'd made it perfectly clear at Zoe's birthday party that the sooner we left, the better.

"Not now, Mom. Later, okay?" There's no need for me to add 'once Zoe goes to bed', my mom already nodding in silent agreement.

The new contract is a far cry from working at Lily's place. While there, I'd been eager to get to the job site each day, especially joining Lily for breakfast in her trailer.

I missed that time with her. Even putting the mind-blowing sex to one side, I'd loved the simple pleasure of holding her tight while we found our equilibrium. Of discussing what was on the punch list for the day, and even talking about Zoe and what she was up to.

Only now do I realize how special it was to have someone to talk through things with. Much as my mom wanted to, she was still my mom. I couldn't be as free with her as I could with Lily.

I'd give anything to go back in time to Zoe's birthday to see if I could change the outcome. While neither Zoe nor Lily would speak of it, something had to have happened. Perhaps if I could work out what it was, I could fix it?

As expected, the day drags. Even though Zac has joined me along with a couple of guys I'd gotten at the veterans' center, there's a subdued air on site. This is mostly down to us working around the client. And while that'd also been the case with Lily, she was happy to roll her sleeves up, whereas our new client works from home.

Zac, however, is happy with the new job, unable to keep his eyes off the woman at the enormous computer in the front room. If I'd looked as obvious as Zac does with his infatuation, it's as well I'm away from Lily.

"Zac, mate, you want to tone it down? Ethan's calling by soon."

He looks briefly in my direction, before his gaze returns to the picture window and the perfect view of Kelly Sanderson, the homeowner.

"Zac!" His head spins back in my direction. "I need you to head into town for some more supplies."

It was something I'd been planning on doing myself, but with him mooning over Kelly like he is, he risks being fired. Zac's too good to lose because of some stupid rule of Ethan's.

He looks ready to argue with me, but soon enough, ditches his tool belt and grabs his keys. A second later and he's holding his hand out, presumably for the list.

"I'll email it through to you."

He's barely left when Ethan arrives, and he doesn't have good news.

"Tomorrow morning? Damn it, Ethan, they said we'd have those windows yesterday."

He doesn't bother replying other than to shrug his shoulders, both of us all too well aware how fickle window manufacturers could be.

A mental check of what we've got that we can work on in the meantime, and I know it's not a lot. "I guess we'll finish up here and join you over at the Finnegan place?"

While I've offered to join the team over at Lily's house, I'm hoping Ethan will turn me down.

"Nah, don't worry about it. We've got it under control. If you and Zac want to tidy up here, you can call it a day. Where is he, by the way?

"I sent him into town to pick up a few things. I'll let him know he can head home after that."

Ethan on his way, the site tidied, and a text sent to Zac to follow up on the email of stuff we'll need along with an order number, and I'm free to leave. A quick goodbye to the homeowner to let her know what's happening, and I'm on my way.

On checking the clock on the dash, I realize if I hurry, I can drop my truck off at mom's and go walk

Zoe home from school. This will be a first for me, and one I'm looking forward to.

It'll be nice to see for myself how she gets on with the other kids. To check they're not being mean to her. While I know my own experiences as a kid are coloring this, I still want to check she's okay.

I needn't have worried, with my daughter soon enveloped by kids, chattering and laughing and talking in a language I don't quite understand. This I can cope with.

What I can't cope with is the mothers moving in on me, especially when the one who strokes my arm is wearing one mother of a wedding ring.

SEVENTEEN

LILY

I've been to Skye High Pies for breakfast every day for the past two weeks. My only plus is the extra pounds I've gained thanks to not being able to resist all the delicious treats on offer.

While some women find it impossible to eat when they're heartbroken, I'm the other way around. Sugar is my drug of choice in situations like this. That and caffeine, although this is mostly to cancel out the nights spent tossing and turning.

It's this very lack of sleep that sees me at Skye High Pies later than usual this morning. Today it's not so much breakfast as an early lunch.

"The usual?" Katie behind the counter has asked before the front door has hissed shut behind me. I nod in return and try my best at smiling, before heading for my favorite table.

It's not the best table on offer, but it's where I feel most comfortable. It's also where I'd sat next to Tyler when we'd gone over the costs all those weeks ago.

I haven't seen so much as a passing glimpse of him since things had ended as badly as they did at Zoe's party. It's also proving impossible to pick up much from the guys at the job site.

Sure, I hear the odd snippet when I'm stripping yet another layer of paint off those vintage cabinets, but that's it.

Of course, I could ring Tyler. However, after the way I'd been so cold with him and Zoe on the day of her party, I'm not sure what sort of response I'd get. My heart having been in pieces, I hadn't been thinking straight.

Rather, I'd wanted them gone so I could lick my wounds and berate the universe yet again, for giving me a body that didn't work.

A moment later, and Katie puts a cup of freshly brewed coffee and a slice of pie on the table. "Here you go, Sugar. Enjoy."

"Thank you. Ah, Katie..."

She stops and turns; her face alight with a readiness to help me, no matter what. Only I can't ask, the words jamming in my throat as that piece of pie never will. "Never mind. It's nothing."

I'd love to ask her if she's seen Tyler. A brief description of him and his tattoos and she'd know exactly who I was talking about. But I can't. Every time we'd been together, part of me couldn't believe a guy that gorgeous would actually choose a curvy girl.

The idea of me asking and her laughing at my delusion chills me to the bone. Not that she's been anything other than friendly. This irrational fear is my issue, not hers. Instead, I concentrate on my pie and coffee, making notes on my phone about things I need to organize for the house.

It's something that'll result in another visit to the hardware store, and I'm dreading it, with the place holding too many memories by far.

And as expected, it's every bit as awful as I'd thought it would be, with memories of Tyler and that little boy hitting me from every angle. While Zoe has her heart set on a little sister, Tyler would be a wonderful dad to a little boy

The only plus to the visit is when I get chatting to an old man in the aisle devoted to cabinet pulls. Apparently, if I cook the existing paint-laden handles in a crock pot with laundry detergent for a few hours, the paint will come right off.

It's a hack that has me leaving with a budget model tucked under one arm.

Even with a lot for me to do back at the house, I don't head straight home. That was never my plan, with me having grabbed some pastries before I'd left the bakery. It's been too long since I visited Alice, mostly down to my still coming to terms with her adoption bombshell.

I still think my nanna should have said something, rather than leave it to a virtual stranger to break the news. Hearing that Alice knew more of my history than I did had hurt.

Despite my ranting and raving, she'd stressed how much Dot loved me. According to her, my nanna never once let the small matter of us not being blood relations impede that. However, it was finding the scrap book amongst the last of my nana's belongings that really brought this home for me.

Newspaper clippings of every event in my life, no matter how inconsequential. Photos of me in school plays and sitting in the 'big chair' at her place, reading yet another of the gorgeous books she'd bought for me.

It was only on flipping over to the last page I'd found the newspaper article that detailed my parent's car accident. It wasn't one I'd ever seen before and I hadn't thought to go looking for it, preferring to bury my past with my family.

Reading it had me sobbing my heart out, with no lessening the grief now that I knew we weren't blood relations. Instead, the loss had been as fresh and strong as ever. Despite our DNA not matching up, they'd been my family in every sense of the word.

My being adopted hadn't mattered one bit. My love for my sister was all-consuming from the moment I'd laid eyes on her at the hospital.

Would Zoe really care if it was the same for the little sister she wants so much? I don't think she would, not if she's like me. I'm parking at the Rose Haven when I realize it wasn't something I could have raised, anyway. Not so early in our relationship. If I'd done that, Tyler would have thought I was some sort of bunny boiler.

"Hey, I know we've only been an item for a little over a month, but I was wondering how you feel about us adopting?"

Even saying it to myself in the car has me snorting in disbelief at this ludicrous proposal. If I'd come out with something like that, the man would have run a mile, and kept going.

This thought clouds my mind on the drive home from the Rose Haven after what had been a late lunch. Distracted as I am, it takes a moment to see that amid a group of moms and kids, there's a man walking along with a little girl. It's Tyler.

The large backpack that dwarves Zoe's small frame says he's walking her home from school, the pair deep in conversation to the exclusion of all else. Even after everything that's happened, I'd give anything to be holding her other hand.

I'm looking in the rear-view mirror when I spot one mom approaching Tyler, her hand coming to rest on his arm possessively. Unable to take my eyes off the scene, next thing I know, I've mounted the curb and blown my front right tire.

I'm still sitting there in shock when Tyler wrenches open my door before crouching down next to me. Meanwhile, Zoe hovers right behind him. "Lily, Lily! Are you okay?"

"I'm, I'm fine." Although having Tyler this close has my heart hammering away and me fighting the impulse to throw myself into his arms. If it weren't for Zoe's presence, I might even surrender.

Then I decide to hell with it, and throw myself into his arms, mortified when I burst into loud sobs. These far outweigh the gravity of my minor accident, although Tyler says nothing other than hugging me back and shushing me.

It's when I feel a small hand hold tight to mine that I really lose it. Some things are worth fighting for, and that includes family in whatever form it takes.

TYLER

Before the mom had reached out and touched me, Zoe had been about to tell me something. This had me turning on the woman, my expression enough to have her taking her hand away as if burned.

Knowing my daughter as well as I do, I've expected a confession for a couple of days now. Experience says that the time it's taking her to get up the nerve to say something means it'll be a doozy.

Like using my mom's best china for a playdate with the mermaid doll Lily had bought her at the aquarium. A playdate that ended with several cups and saucers being smashed, although only thanks to enthusiasm.

I forget all this when I hear a loud bang from farther up the road. The minute I recognize Lily's car, I take off, dragging Zoe in my wake. Even with her little legs slowing us down, I'm soon enough opening the car door, desperate to see if the woman I love is okay.

She is, but there's no missing that she's upset with her tears doing the same to me. And I'm not alone, with Zoe now hugging my back and joining me in telling

Lily that it'll be okay, that she hadn't meant what she'd said.

It isn't until I've changed the blown tire, dropped Zoe at my mom's, and am driving Lily home I recall my daughter's admission. And in hindsight, there'd also been no missing Zoe's remorse when she'd hugged Lily as if she never wanted to let go.

Unfortunately, on pulling up at Lily's place, I'm dismayed to see Ethan's truck out front. Much as I want to talk to her about this while it's fresh in my mind, I can't. Not without risking my job.

And now that I've seen the cost of some of the add-ons offered by Zoe's new school, I can't afford for that to happen. It's something that has me helping Lily out of her car and then leaving as soon as I can.

The only plus is that with Coogan's Break being reasonably small, it doesn't take me long to walk back to my mom's place. While it hadn't been possible to ask to Lily what my daughter was talking about, there's nothing to stop me from going straight to the source.

I'm all for interrogating my daughter until I find her lying face down on her bed. She's wearing the mermaid tail Lily had given her for her birthday, her small body wracked with tears.

No sooner have I sat on the edge of her bed than she flips over and throws herself into my arms. "Shush, shush, it's okay. It'll be okay. Remember, a problem shared is a problem halved."

She's shaking her head even before she can get the words out. "No, it won't! I ruined it. It's all my fault."

She's now crying hard enough that I worry she'll make herself sick. It's also loud enough for my mom to pop her head through the door. When she sees Zoe in my arms, she retreats, closing the door after her.

It's not until Zoe's tears have subsided to the occasional hiccup that she talks, and even then, it makes little sense. At least until I hear her say, "I know you said not to tell her what I wanted for my birthday, but I wanted it so bad, Daddy."

This has me working my way through her birthday wish list, with this extensive enough that I'd had to say no to more than half-a-dozen pink, glittery things. It's only when I think of the big-ticket item that she'd added at the end that my eyes widen in shock.

It would sure as hell explain why Lily had withdrawn like she did. Everything had been perfect when I went into the trailer to make our root beer floats. I'd definitely been gone long enough for my daughter to tell Lily about her wanting a little sister for her birthday.

And it was the one thing Lily couldn't give her. I'm then wondering why Lily had said nothing when Zoe stutters out, "I told her you said I shouldn't say anything, and she said it'd be our girly secret."

Damn it, I knew Lily well enough that she'd never rat out my daughter. "Oh, Zoe girl." I say nothing else, simply dropping a kiss atop her head. There's nothing I can say, not without heaping even more guilt on my little girl.

And yet I know I can't leave it like this. Being with Lily had me happier than I'd been since before I lost Jade. Maybe even happier with us definitely having our trials over the years. I even wonder if Jade hadn't fallen pregnant, whether we'd still be together.

Now what I need to work out is how the hell I put this right. I can't very well rock up to Lily's trailer and ask her how she feels about adoption. It's way too soon for that sort of talk.

At least I think it is. It's something that has me disentangling myself from my daughter's arms and tucking her blankie around her. Back out in the hallway, I find my mom hovering.

"Mom, I need your advice on something."

Hah, if the woman looked worried over breakfast, it's nothing compared to her concern now.

"Relax, it's nothing bad. At least I hope not."

EIGHTEEN

LILY

After dropping me off, Tyler hadn't waited around, with the last I saw of him being him marching back the way we'd come.

As in a daze as I'd been on the drive home, I couldn't even tell you how far away his mom's house was from mine. Hopefully not too far.

A distracted wave to the Lucky Break crew and I hurry through the orchard to the trailer. Despite my telling Tyler I was okay, that tire blow-out was a real shock, especially coming as it did so soon after seeing him with that woman.

No doubt my idiocy will be something they'll have a good laugh about later. It's a thought that has my tears threatening by the time I unlock the door and stumble inside.

All I want to do is climb into bed and curl up in a ball. Which is exactly what I do, falling into a deep sleep for the first time in days. On waking with a start, I'm unsure how much time has elapsed, although the gloom in the trailer says I've slept longer than I have in weeks.

I'm drowning my sorrows in a pint of chocolate ice cream when there's a tap on the trailer door. As unexpected as this is, I have trouble swallowing the large spoonful I've just taken.

It has to be Tyler, because other than Ethan coming over to ask about my final tile choice, no-one else has ventured back here.

This sees me shoving the tub of ice cream, complete with spoon, in the freezer. A quick swipe of my mouth with the back of my hand, and I'm as ready as I'll ever be.

My preparations are a failure of epic proportions when, on opening the door, my reaction to Tyler is such that I freeze. While my first instinct is to step back so he can enter the small space, I can't do it. The place already haunts me with memories of our special times together.

Instead, I join him in the clearing next to the trailer, the space now outfitted with a couple of wicker chairs I'd picked up at a yard sale. My "please, have a seat," is more down to the manners drummed into me by Nanna Dot than any wish to prolong this agony.

Unsteady on my feet, I drop into the chair that's closest to me, glad of the support. Only after Tyler has sat do I realize I haven't offered him anything to drink. A beat and I decide it's better if I don't. The sooner I get this over with, the better.

How I'll go about that, I'm not sure. I hadn't thought to rehearse this scene. Part of me didn't think it would be necessary. Not with that other woman now in the picture.

"How are you? Are you okay? What happened with the car?" Tyler leans forward in his chair, waiting for me to respond. Something I'm having trouble with.

Because he'd driven my car back here, I can't even use the excuse that the steering was playing up, and it was this that had me hitting the curb.

"Just a silly mistake. My fault. I shouldn't read texts when I'm driving. I should pay more attention." It's only running out of lettuce that puts an end to the word salad I'm flinging in his direction. "How's Zoe? Is she enjoying school?"

As a diversion, it's clunky, but it's one I know will work, having seen how Tyler dotes on his daughter. Sure enough, he proudly tells of the number of gold stars she's already racked up, and how many friends she's making.

And then, despite my brain yelling SHUT UP, SHUT UP, SHUT UP, I have to do just the opposite.

"It looks like she isn't the only one who's making new friends. I'm so pleased for you." I'm not really, but I'd like to preserve some small shred of self-esteem if possible.

However, rather than looking as if he's off the hook, he looks confused. "She looks like a lovely lady, and her little girl was cute as a button."

Despite my shock, I couldn't help but notice when the mystery woman walked past my car. Her little girl was a gorgeous little thing who'd waved gaily at Zoe before skipping off after her mom.

Tyler's daughter deserved a sister like that, and maybe even more siblings. In the months before the car accident, my mom had even hinted the family might get bigger. The only thing I'll never know is whether my parents were planning on having another kid, or adopting again.

Despite my Nanna Dot showering me with love and declaring us a team, it hadn't been the same as living with my 'own' family. There'd always been something missing, and I wouldn't wish that on Zoe.

I also wouldn't wish it on Tyler, with his life not sounding the best after his dad did a runner. Sometimes even love isn't enough, and if anyone deserves the perfect family, it's those two.

Tyler briefly shakes his head as if to clear his thoughts. "Lily, what on earth are you talking about?"

Now I'm the one who's confused. Hadn't I made myself clear? Hadn't I just wished him well with his new relationship? That woman and her daughter would give Zoe and Tyler everything they wanted. That's what he wanted, wasn't it?

I'm still wondering how I can make it clearer for him without ripping my heart to shreds when he roars with laughter. He does his best to hide this with a coughing fit, but I'm not fooled. On looking up from where I've been bunching my dress in my lap, I'm surprised to see his eyes alight with suppressed laughter.

"She's been asking about you." He laughs briefly, before adding, "Incessantly."

Shock wracks my body. How could he be so cruel? All he had to do was stay away from here and let whatever it was we'd had die a natural death. Much as I want to storm to my feet and kick him out, I'm incapable.

"She misses you. Asks after you every day."

Now I'm the one who's shaking their head, hoping to fire a few synapses. "Zoe?"

He nods before lurching out of his chair and over to kneel in front of me. Once there, he takes my hands in his, thumbs rubbing the backs of them in soothing circles.

"Lily, if you were talking about the mom who was hitting on me when you drove past, she's married. There's also the minor issue that it's not her I love."

TYLER

If not for my chat with Zoe after I'd walked home from Lily's earlier, I'd have been completely in the dark at this stage. Add in the sage advice from my mom, and I know what I'm doing.

Well, not exactly, but as much as I could hope for in a situation like this.

As surprising as my daughter's confession that she'd told Lily she wanted a baby sister, was my mom being fully on-board with the idea of adoption. According to her, "There are too many babies in this world not being properly cared for".

And this without her even having met Lily. Her, "If you love her, then so do I," had floored me, with me only recently admitting to myself that's what I felt for Lily.

And yet it's now beyond doubt, even if it's still early days.

However, my confidence comes unstuck when Lily earnestly tells me that 'she' looks like a lovely lady. It takes a second for me to realize who it is that she's talking about, with my responding laughter purely down to relief

As I kneel in front of her, I know the only way I'll discover if Lily feels the same way is if I come right out and say it.

"Lily, I love you." This is as far as I get, my mouth now as dry as the outer suburbs of Las Vegas. Only by clearing my throat, am I able to continue. It's an action that has my throat as raw as my emotions.

"Zoe told me what she said about her birthday wish, and we had a long talk."

It had been one that left my daughter surprised, with her thinking every woman could be a mommy. She'd then said something that left me the one surprised.

"If I can't have a little sister, can I have a mommy?" She'd then looked up at me, her eyes bright with tears, and whispered, "Can we have Lily?"

Unable to speak, I'd simply nodded.

I'm no longer sure of the promise I'd made to my daughter, with Lily's silence leaving me in doubt.

"Lily?" Her silence is worrying, and she's back to looking at her lap, in a move designed to avoid eye contact.

How could I have gotten it so wrong?

"I... I can't..."

Her then running out of words has me rocking back on my heels and wondering what it is she can't do. Love me? Have kids? Commit? What?

"I can't have babies, you know that. I can't deny Zoe a little sister. Losing my own nearly destroyed me when I was a kid."

Ah, so here's the rub. Relief floods me.

"Lily, I know it's early days, but Zoe has already said she's happy with us adopting, although only if she gets to help choose." I'm unable to stop a snort of laughter at the memory of that request.

"I tried explaining that it wasn't like getting a new puppy or a kitten, but she didn't want to hear about it."

When I'd left for Lily's, my daughter was busy drawing a picture of her ideal little sister. I can't wait to see what the adoption people think when we turn up, slap that down on the counter, and say, "We'll have one of these, please."

Lost in my thoughts, it takes a second to realize Lily is looking at me teary-eyed, but more promising is the wobbly smile that's forming. Then, just as she'd done when I'd opened the car door after her accident, she throws herself into my arms. Instinctively, I grab hold of her, determined never to let go.

In between kissing her hair, I tell her how it's been. "I've missed you so much, Lily. I've missed our mornings. Our breakfasts together."

I don't progress any further with my list, more interested in pure love than making love, although I know that will change.

Our physical connection was one of the strongest I'd ever experienced.

It's Lily who instigates our kiss, her tongue exploring my mouth as if for the first time. And I get why she's being tentative. With me having declared my love for her, it's as if we're starting over.

The only thing I'm unsure of is whether she feels the same way as I do. While I long for a proper family as much as my daughter, it still has to be right. Much as it devastated Lily to lose her little sister so young, the same would be true for Zoe if Lily and I got together, only to break up.

Hadn't this been what had held me back from committing to a relationship in all these years? Or was it I'd never found someone who I'd risk it all for?

It's this that has me gently breaking our embrace. If I'm to get the words out, I need some distance to allow myself to think straight. It's at this point I don't realize how I'm supposed to go about it. My saying let's be friends would surely kill off any connection we've got. And anyway, that's the last thing I want. This has me thinking back to how we'd met, our introduction unorthodox in the extreme.

A moment later and I'm on my feet and gently pulling Lily to hers. I follow this up by executing a courtly bow. "Hello, I'm Tyler Pierce, single dad, and a bit of a bad boy in my youth. I'm a supervisor at Lucky Break Construction."

Lily is quick to catch on, her laughter brightening the clearing even more than the strings of lights that are new since I was last here. In response to my bow, she curtsies, even holding the skirts of her dress out to the sides.

"I'm pleased to meet you, Tyler Pierce. I'm Lily Finnegan, divorcee, ex dental hygienist and newbie house flipper. Oh, and I love your teeth!"

This last pronouncement soon has my laughter ringing out with hers.

After our official introduction, I have no reservations about stepping forward and pulling her into a tight embrace. My lips cover hers, her mouth opening in response, telling me the formal part of the evening is well and truly over.

NINETEEN

LILY

As Tyler's lips move over mine, it's as if the past couple of weeks never happened. And yet we're so much farther along, at least in so far as our emotions go.

Mitchell had often told me he loved me in the early days of our courtship. However, he'd never said it with the same passion and vulnerability as Tyler just displayed.

No, it was as if Mitchell said it because he was supposed to, not because he actually believed it. I then have to rid myself of the fleeting thought of him declaring his love for that dental assistant of his.

As if sensing my withdrawal, Tyler gently bites my bottom lip, the resultant spark flooding my body before shooting out the top of my head. On its way, it's hit every nerve ending on offer, with my body now alight with a burning need.

Even better is when this need scorches all memories of my ex. Now all I can think of is Tyler and what he's doing to me. And as wonderful as it is, it's still not enough.

I break the kiss, waiting for him to focus. "Come, it's getting late." There's an immediate flash of disappointment in his eyes, although it disappears the moment that I tug him toward the trailer.

There's only one place I want Tyler Pierce tonight, and that's in my bed. Okay, and maybe under the stars. It is a beautiful night.

Minutes later and we're both naked, the sight of Tyler's arousal sparking my own as always. There's something primal about being able to affect a man like this, of having him on the edge, of losing it.

There's also no doubting the love in his eyes as he

gazes at me. While I haven't told him yet, I know my love for him is just as strong.

I just can't bring myself to say it. Not yet. Once I do that, I'll be making a commitment I'm not sure I can keep. I'm still not comfortable about foisting myself on Tyler and Zoe, given my inability to fulfill my primary role as a woman.

For all Tyler says that he and Zoe are okay with adoption, it's not that simple. It might not happen for years, if ever. Times had changed from when my parents adopted me.

If there was even an outside chance I could conceive, then I might risk it. However, with my womb a crisscross of scar tissue thanks to the until-recently undiagnosed endometriosis, that will never happen.

It's something that hurts even more than all those years of being told by doctor after doctor that the pain was down to women's issues. The most common remedy prescribed was for me to 'suck it up' and get on with my life.

If only it were that easy.

Desperate to move on to happier thoughts, I step forward, bringing myself hard up against Tyler. And it works, and then some, his swollen shaft nudging my stomach, his large hands cupping my breasts, his thumbs stroking my nipples.

It's an incendiary combination that has me gripping his length, desperate to be closer still, to have him fill me over and over, to complete me.

Soon enough, I get my wish, when he lowers me to the bed and follows me down.

After kissing me hard enough to take my breath away, he runs his tongue down the column of my throat, leaving a trail of fire in his wake.

I feel a brief flash of desolation when he lifts his head, but this soon disappears. After rasping one nipple with his tongue, he moves on to the other. As he continues his exploration of my body, the cool night air wraps itself around my still damp nipples, puckering them.

I've not had time to enjoy the sensation when Tyler's tongue hits my core and my hips arch with no input from me. Not content, he peels me wide before blowing gently on my little nubbin.

It's a technique that has me squirming and desperately trying to open myself to him further, my legs splayed wide. It's something he takes full advantage of when, after licking his thumb, he runs it over my pearl and down through my cleft.

There's no need for him to lick his thumb further with me already wet with need. Wet enough, he can plunge his thumb deep inside me with no resistance. The same is true when he replaces it with one, and then two, of his large fingers.

His then imitating the act of making love only using his digits is enough to have me trembling with need. Tyler then leaning down and sucking hard on my nubbin has me close to going over the edge. Too close.

"Tyler! Stop!"

This demand has him lifting his head, his face a picture of concern that I'm not enjoying it. However, after a brief smile to assuage his concerns, I add, "It's wonderful, but I want you deep inside me when I come."

I'm not used to asking for what I want like this, especially not in the bedroom. But I've wanted nothing as much as I want Tyler filling me when my body shatters.

"As you wish."

He doesn't hurry though, working his way back up my body, keeping me just on the edge, just hanging on by a thread.

Him sliding into me is as poetry, so easily is it achieved. We truly fit together like two halves of a puzzle. And then he moves and all thoughts of puzzles flee.

Now all I can think about is how he stretches me, my body aware of every silken inch of him as he fills me over and over.

And yet I want to be closer still, something that has me wrapping my legs around behind him. I want him filling me completely.

Only when he speaks do I find out what's been missing.

"Damn it, Lily. I love you. I love you so much."

His words, interspersed with that slow in and out he has down to a fine art, are enough to have me over the edge. I don't go quietly though.

"Tyler, I love you, too. I love you so much, it hurts."

Everything else I've got to say after this is incoherent as the enormity of my declaration thrums through me. It's as if declaring my true feelings for this wonderful man has made our love-making even more impactful, but it has.

And yet, as Tyler finally succumbs to his own release, I've never felt so vulnerable in all my life. Not even when I was breaking the news to Mitchell that I'd never be able to have children.

He hadn't taken the news well, declaring our five-year marriage a complete waste of his time. His rejection, coming as it had when I was still in the hospital following laparoscopy to remove yet more scar tissue, had been devastating.

I suspect it was also the moment he'd started planning to replace me.

Perhaps it's this that has me unable to believe that Tyler, and especially Zoe, will take me on, even knowing of my shortcomings.

As if sensing my worries, on lying beside me, Tyler places a reverent kiss on my forehead, and then my lips, before holding me tight.

With my head pressed against his solid chest, there's no missing that his heartbeat is even faster than mine. By the time sleep claims us, our hearts are perfectly in sync.

TYLER

On waking the following morning, I take a second to work out where I am. Then, the only thing in no doubt is that I love the woman snuggling up to me more than life itself. Even better is that I know she feels the same way.

So why then do I feel like the other shoe is about to drop?

I know Lily has reservations, but they're nothing we can't face together. I'd told her this after we'd made love a second time in the middle of the night. Yes, adoption can be difficult, but it's not impossible.

There were also a lot of kids in the foster system who were crying out for a wonderful home, if only for a temporary respite. So long had we talked of the pros and cons that it was close to four o'clock before we fell asleep again.

I've come to no conclusions as to my anxiety when there's a loud pounding on the door of the trailer. Ethan follows this up by bellowing my name.

Ah, that'll be it. Next to me, Lily struggles to rouse herself.

"Tyler Pierce, you get your sorry ass out here. Now!"

While my boss wants me out there pronto, there isn't a chance I'm facing him naked. Not if there's any hope of saving my job. I've no sooner thought this than I realize that where Lily is concerned, it's a sacrifice I'm prepared to make.

Sick of scurrying around, keeping our relationship quiet, I want to show the woman I love off to the world, to my family and friends. There isn't a chance I want anyone thinking I'm ashamed of her.

"Hold your horses. I'll be out in a second."

Much as I get along well with my boss, I've no plans to push it by opening that door only wearing a smile. Not with my potentially buying a solitaire soon. And definitely not with Zoe having just started school.

I wasn't kidding when I told Lily that kids were expensive. They are frighteningly so with school supplies that are acceptable to a five-year-old girl. I'm thinking about all of this while dragging on my jeans and t-shirt.

Beside me, Lily struggles into the dress she'd been wearing last night, eschewing her bra and panties in preference for haste. I'm not sure why she's bothering to get dressed. Ethan isn't yelling for her to go out there.

On exiting the trailer, I find Ethan standing in the middle of the clearing, his arms crossed, his lips tight. I don't think I've ever seen him this angry. I don't get it. His rule is stupid, especially when I care about Lily enough that I'm already thinking about making things permanent.

Ethan glares at me, drawing air in hard enough that his nostrils flare. Sheesh, all I need is a red cape to face down this bull.

"I don't ask much of you guys. Turn up on time, do the work, fix your mistakes..." He steps forward, before gritting out, "But number one, and you damn well know it, is don't screw the clients."

Everything he says is true, but I take exception to him saying I'm simply screwing Lily. Nothing could be further from the truth. While the fury in my belly is slow to burn, it soon erupts with me now every bit as angry as my boss.

It's at this point that Lily steps up next to me, sliding her arm around my waist, my arm automatically matching hers. For the first time, we're facing the world as a couple.

Wow, if I thought Ethan was angry before, it's nothing compared to now.

"Ethan, don't you think it's hypocritical to ask your team members not to fraternize with clients?" Lily falls silent while apparently waiting for her words to take effect, although I don't know why they would.

He's still glaring at us when she adds, "Word at the rest home is that you were working for your now-wife when you got together. Is it true you put the *man* in handy man?"

While Ethan looks to be ready to yell at me some more, he doesn't appear capable. Instead, he's lost for words, his mouth mimicking that of a goldfish.

However, Lily still has a lot to say. "And I object to you saying that Tyler is screwing me, as you so delicately put it, when, in fact, I'm screwing him."

After this shock, she disengages herself from my arms and huffs back inside the trailer.

Rather than continue to berate me now that Lily has gone, all Ethan says is, "I want you over at the Sanderson place by eight-thirty or I'm docking your pay." After this vain attempt to gain the upper hand, he spins around and marches off.

"I'll just grab my boots and be on my way."

On opening the trailer door, I'm still in a bit of a daze. When he'd shouted my name earlier, never in a million years could I have foreseen this outcome.

Lily is waiting for me just inside the door. After throwing her arms around me, she reaches up on tiptoe and hits me with a kiss, passionate enough to clear my thoughts immediately.

It's also a move that has her hard up against me, reminding me she's naked under that dress, although it's gone soon enough. I don't bother undressing completely myself. We've only got fifteen or twenty minutes. And I want them to be the best of Lily's life.

So good, in fact, that I have to walk out to my truck still holding my boots. Ethan didn't stipulate I turn up at the other job completely dressed, now did he?

On climbing out of my truck at the Sanderson place, I'm whistling to myself. I'm happy with this new direction in my life, happy to have Lily willing to fight my fights. At least this one time. Damn it, after hearing how her ex treated her, I'm tempted to show the guy some dentistry skills of my own.

As sure as I am of the air I breathe, no one will ever mistreat Lily like that again. Not while I've got anything to say about it.

TWENTY

LILY

The rest of the flip passes in a blur, the house coming alive thanks to the Lucky Break team. I've also come to trust in my choices around design and changes to the floor plan.

While it had caused a lot of grumbling and head scratching from the team, the changes have been worth it. Certainly, the house flows better than it ever did now that it's more open-plan than was popular back in the day.

Silly, but the thing I'm proudest of is those kitchen cabinets. After I'd removed all the layers of paint and spent hours sanding, the wood now gleams.

And dang if that old guy wasn't on the money with his crock pot trick. While it's possible to buy reproduction vintage hardware, it's never as good as the original. It's definitely a hack I'll use in the future, with me more determined than ever to make a go of flipping houses.

Just as I've moved on from Mitchell, I've moved on from the career he'd suggested I take up not long after we'd met. As infatuated as I'd been with him, I'd given no thought to changing schools mid-year.

Thinking back, I should have stuck with the design course as I'd wanted to. What an idiot I'd been to choose dental impressions over dental moldings, and all for the love of that two-timing creep.

It's yet another thing I love about Tyler. He doesn't want to change me at all. If I'm happy, then he's happy. Not that this stops us from discussing things that affect both of us.

He's definitely a breath of fresh air in that department after years of knowing it was easier to say, "Yes, of course," to any of Mitchell's many *suggestions*.

The other thing that had pleased me was when Zac and Tyler returned to the site after finishing up that other job. This meant Tyler and I could have lunch together as often as we wanted to, with Ethan unable to say a thing about it.

It hadn't taken long for word to get out about my showdown with the boss over his stupid rule. Zac, in particular, appeared overjoyed, immediately packing up his lunch while muttering something about needing to collect supplies in town.

As we sit on the top step and watch Zac's truck disappearing down the road, Tyler nudges me with his shoulder. "I wouldn't mind collecting some supplies in town."

There's no missing his hidden message with him having told me all about Zac's infatuation with Kelly Sanderson, the client at the job they'd not long finished.

"Now that you mention it, there was something I wanted to pick up in town, but it's very heavy, so I'll probably need your help."

There's no stopping Tyler's laughter in response to this, although he calms down enough to splutter out. "If it's the model I'm thinking of, it's also got some length and width to it."

"That's the one. Luckily, I've got the perfect spot for it."

"Jeez, you two, get a room, will you?"

I've no need to turn around to know this complaint is from Cole, although he's got a point.

"Tyler, you heard the man." I'm on my feet a second later, racing down the front steps with Tyler right behind me.

Cole's, "Aww freaking hell, I didn't mean it!" follows in our wake, but it's too late with me already opening the door of Tyler's truck. He's not far behind, with us leaving in a squeal of tires soon after.

We're in the shower at his place in town, the lease still having a couple of months to run, when Tyler stops briefly with his lathering of me. "Don't forget, we've got Zoe's school play this afternoon."

In order to clear my head enough to respond sensibly, I turn off the hot tap, resulting in us being blasted with freezing water. This both dampens my arousal and rinses me clean of any remaining suds. It's brutal, but effective.

"That's today? I thought it was tomorrow?"

Tyler wrenches off the cold water before looking at me sheepishly. "I told you they'd had to change it, didn't I?"

By now, I'm out of the shower and wrapping a towel around myself. Only once my hands are dry, do I grab my phone off the kitchen counter and open my calendar.

There, as clear as a bell, is Zoe's play, set for three o'clock tomorrow.

"Tyler!" After slamming my phone down, I rub myself dry, conscious I need to get home and tidy up properly. This will be the first time I've been to a school event. I don't want to rock up looking as though I've just had toe-curling sex, even if it's true.

"Sorry, I thought I'd told you about it. We're not due there for an hour and a half. We'll be okay."

As I struggle into my clothes, my still damp skin making this nigh on impossible, I don't share his confidence. The only plus in all of this is that I'd had my hair bundled up for the shower.

Soon enough we're on our way back to my place, with Tyler even turning the truck into the driveway and going as far as he can. The second he applies the brakes, I'm out of the car.

It isn't just that I need to change into something that will have me blending with all those moms. I want to call into a florist and get Zoe some flowers to celebrate this milestone.

The other thing I'm conscious of is looking nice in front of Tyler's mom. It doesn't matter that the woman is as down to earth as they come. I want to make a good impression.

All this has me a bundle of nerves when we pull up outside the school with minutes to spare. Most of this is thanks to the florist taking as long with the bouquet as Mother Nature took to grow the flowers.

We meet Sarah, Tyler's mom, outside the hall doors with her relief at spotting us, only reinforcing how late we really are. It's also something that sees us sitting in the very back row.

Too far back to see much of what's going on, and too far back for the third princess in from the left to see we've made it. As I sit with the small, and very pink, bouquet in my lap, I vow to make it up to Zoe.

TYLER

I'm in bliss as I sit with Lily on one side and my mom on the other. Meanwhile, my daughter is up on stage showing a complete lack of talent for singing and dancing.

This doesn't bother me with her already showing herself to be smart as a whip with subjects like writing and math. And despite what her teacher says, there's plenty of time for her to decide what she wants to be when she grows up.

The play is both excruciating and hilarious. However, the humor is less intentional, and more to do with the individuality of some cast members and their desire to improvise.

Forty-five agonizing minutes have passed before I spot the scruffy little boy Lily and I had seen walking home from school. On stage, he's a prince among his fellow students, commanding the stage as he never would the classroom.

Doubtless, the ability to play a part like that will be down to life experience. For kids like him, if they could pretend they were anything other than what they were, it could save a world of pain.

I knew, having spent enough time as a kid, acting like I didn't care that my clothes were threadbare and my shoes had holes in them. Shrug it off with enough bravado, and you can sell it to anyone, especially the bullies.

Thankfully, that hadn't been an issue after I'd shot up in middle school, towering over those who'd made elementary school pure hell for me. It was something that also allowed me to save my younger brothers from the same fate.

There isn't a chance anyone would be stupid enough to pick a fight with them these days, with them just as tall and broad as I am.

And speaking of pure hell, another fifteen agonizing minutes pass before the entire 'cast', AKA every kid in the school, appears on stage for a standing ovation.

While every parent present is proud, we're also delirious to be standing after an hour in what had proven to be damned uncomfortable chairs. It also gives me a chance to wave wildly, allowing Zoe to spot me. There are pluses to being as tall as I am.

Next to me, Lily is doing her best to pass the small bouquet in front of me to my mom. My mom just as forcefully pushes it back with a hissed, "No, Lily, it's only right you take it up to her."

Next thing I know, Lily is trying to foist it onto me. There isn't a chance a great, lumbering fool like me is traipsing up on stage as other parents are. I smile as encouragingly as I can, before adding, "Off you go. She'll love seeing you."

And she will, with my daughter asking after Lily every night before bed. Zoe is even more besotted with Lily after many an outing for the three of us.

A huff of annoyance, and Lily eases her way out of our row and into the center aisle. On watching her walking up to the stage clasping that small bouquet, my heart sticks in my throat.

It must be an emotion my mom shares, with her grabbing onto my arm as though it's the only thing keeping her upright. A glance down and I'm surprised to see her eyes are wet with tears. My mom never cries, like ever.

Well, she did the day dad left, but not once since then.

Up on stage, Lily reverently presents the bouquet to Zoe, before bending and kissing my daughter on both cheeks. Cheeks that are pink with delight that Lily has given her the one thing me or my mum can't.

And that's a mother figure who matches the others on stage. A second later, and Zoe throws her arms around Lily, doing a great job of crushing the flowers.

Lily returns the embrace with as much fervor, leading Zoe off the stage and down the aisle toward us. To the casual observer, they could be mistaken for mother and daughter, with Zoe a mini-me to Lily.

By now my smile muscles are hurting, but I wouldn't have it any other way.

After I scoop Zoe up, flowers and all, she wraps her arms tight around my neck. "I was worried you'd forgotten."

This has me leaning back enough that I can look her in the eye. "And miss the performance of a life-time? Heck no!" My daughter knows me well enough to burst out laughing at this declaration.

We're out front of the hall when she whispers, "I was terrible, wasn't I?" Any worries about my daughter's soul being crushed disappear when she giggles.

I'm laughing, too, when I comment, "You were appalling!"

Lily and my mom are quick to catch on with Lily declaring it to be, "The worst play I've ever seen".

There's barely a beat before Zoe, my mom and I reply in concert, "Ah, but you have seen it!" The captain of the Black Pearl would have been proud of us.

On seeing a small boy dragged by us, our mood changes as we watch his father wrench on the threadbare collar of his son's shirt to control him.

"What an effing waste of time. Don't know why I had to go to that freak show." The asshat follows this up by shoving his son forward, to the point the boy comes close to losing his footing.

Something in me snaps, a deep anger bubbling to the surface. No kid deserves to be treated like that. Next to me, Lily and my mom share my fury, their bodies tense and ready for action.

Without hesitation, I slide Zoe to the ground and take off after the guy, my meaty hand landing on his shoulder. Much as I want to teach him a lesson, I need to test the waters first. "Your kid. He's really got some skills there," I say through gritted teeth.

The guy blinks in my direction for a second, and I can see the coldness in his eyes. "Hah, you mean Lucas? Like hell he's mine. Only reason me and the missus took him on was for the money. Kid's an effing waste of space," he sneers.

My anger surges in response to his callous words, but short of making a scene, I can't do anything else, although Lily soon steps in. With a fierce determination, she walks over to the young boy and tells him he did fantastic.

Her words are like a ray of sunshine in the darkness, and the boy's eyes light up briefly before flickering out.

As the pair drives away in the guy's fully tricked-out truck, I wrap my arms around my girls, holding them close. While the sadness of the scene lingers, it's shown me how lucky I am to have these amazing women in my life.

"I need something to get rid of the foul taste, after that," says Lily, her voice a mix of sadness and anger.

"Ice cream?" says Zoe, with anticipation.

My mom nods in agreement. "Yes, and we'll need chocolate sauce on top. A lot."

As we make our way to my truck, I feel a sense of hope that had been missing for so long. Despite the cruelty in the world, there is love and kindness to be found, and I know my future is bright with these wonderful women by my side.

EPILOGUE

SIX MONTHS LATER

LILY

Out in front of the latest flip, I marvel at how smoothly things are going. It's a far cry from when I'd flipped that first place, the place Tyler, Zoe and I now call home.

And yes, of course, there's a white picket fence out front.

After checking on the last delivery of the day and indeed the week, I make my way over to the Airstream, that now doubles as a staff break room. That's when it's not being used for family vacations.

Zoe loves going away in what she calls the shiny house. I love her so much. There are times I'm sure my heart will burst. Certainly, she's as close to me as I imagine a child of my own would be.

I then bring myself up short. She is my child in every way that counts, with me at last able to understand adoption from my parents' perspective. They had loved me wholeheartedly; I know that now.

This had gone a long way toward ridding me of the heartache I'd felt when Alice first broke the news of my adoption. Any retrospection disappears when I pop my head through the Airstream's door.

Packed as it is with a half-dozen Lucky Break Construction crew, it's a veritable bachelorette party in the making. Of course, I only have eyes for one of the gorgeous men enjoying a well-earned beer at the end of another busy week.

"The windows are here. I'm off to pick Zoe up from your mom's. See you at home later?"

Rather than stay where he is, Tyler puts his beer down on the Formica table and lurches to his feet. He soon joins me outside, walking me out to my truck.

Long gone is my impractical car, replaced by a truck

capable of carrying everything I need. It's also fully kitted out to tow the trailer.

After I unlock my door, Tyler pulls me in for an embrace that belies the fact we'll be seeing each other again in an hour. He's kissing me like his life depends on it when my phone pings.

It's not enough to break our kiss, although when his phone sounds almost immediately after, it is. For us both to get messages at the same time says that whatever it is, it's important.

This has me rummaging through my purse, desperate to find my phone. If anything has happened to Zoe...

Next to me, Tyler has already grabbed his phone out of the back pocket of his jeans and is scrolling through the message. Soon enough, I'm similarly engaged. For a second neither of us reacts, but soon enough we both break into broad grins.

It's taken months of complete courses, training, and badgering social services, but finally, we've got the news we've been waiting for. Only on scrolling further down the email, do I think to check what the time is. It's only three-thirty, with the boys always finishing early on a Friday.

My phone dumped back in my purse. I grab the front of Tyler's t-shirt, pulling him toward me, all fired up. "We have to get him this afternoon. I don't want that boy spending another night with that awful man."

There's no doubting Tyler agrees with him already running around to the passenger side. "You drive, I'll ring mom and tell her what's happening."

We don't have long to wait at social services for the waste of space foster dad to arrive with Lucas, the newest member of our little blended family. It's amazing how quickly the authorities had pulled the boy after they caught the foster dad drunk and naked in the Founders Park fountain. I guess we owe Cole some beers for that stunt, because it's got his fingerprints all over it.

That the guy is angry to be losing his meal ticket shows when he shoves the boy out of his truck while they're still in the parking lot. A plastic bag of belongings follows, landing hard next to the kid. The deadbeat then drives off without a backward glance, leaving Tyler rigid with rage, and me not far behind him.

Unfortunately, as newly minted foster parents, we can't act on our fury. All we can do is make sure

Lucas has the best life, with it having let him down enough already.

TYLER

Inside, they usher the three of us into a small office, with Lily and I sitting on either side of an obviously nervous Lucas. And who can blame the boy? According to Marta, our case manager, the boy's been through home after home since his mom died of an overdose.

I'm hoping us taking him on will put an end to that. The thing that gives us the best chance of success is that we're not doing it for the money. We're doing it for the kid and that makes a big difference.

We're busy with paperwork when there's a tap on the door, with Marta getting up to answer it while we keep checking and signing. Meanwhile, Lucas sits as a stone, apparently scared to move for fear of what?

Being smacked around the back of the head?

My concentration being what it is, I take a moment to realize I can smell my mom's perfume. A quick look over my shoulder and I spot her just inside the door, along with Zoe.

Soon enough Lily notices the pair, her surprise clear. Then she nods. "It's only right you're here for this."

Zoe and my mom sit quietly on a small bench just inside the door. Meanwhile, Lily and I have a last check of the paperwork before passing it over to Marta.

She's skimming down the page, her finger tapping our entries as she checks them. Then she stops, her brow creased in a frown.

"It says here that you're still living together. That you're not married. Is that correct? I prefer parents be married."

This is a surprise, with our living arrangement not an issue for everyone else we've dealt with. It even says on their website that couples living together can foster. I suspect the marriage angle is Marta's own hangup rather than anything to do with department protocol.

Honestly, if they'll farm kids out to the asshole who just left, why is the starchy woman behind the desk now balking at us? It's just as well I've come prepared, something that soon has me on my feet.

A moment later and I'm next to Lily's chair, something that has her looking at me, obviously wondering what on earth I'm up to. "Tyler Pierce, we are not leaving. They've approved everything. A marriage certificate is only a piece of paper. Family is about more than that."

She then turns and squeezes Lucas's shoulder as if to say, "I've got this."

By the time she's done that and turned back to face me, I'm down on one knee, a small ring box clasped in my sweaty hand. I've never been as nervous in my entire life, but I want this to be right.

"Lily Finnegan, will you do me the honor of becoming my wife?" I look briefly at Marta. "And not just because it'll make her happy, but because I love you more than I'd have thought possible."

While I wait on her response, the room is all but silent, with no-one daring to breathe. The only sound is a faint rustling, which I put down to the air-conditioning.

A second later and Lily throws herself into my arms, as is her habit.

"Yes! Yes! Of course, I'll marry you, Tyler Pierce."

To an accompaniment of cheering, I seal our engagement with a kiss, even if it's nowhere as passionate as I'd like. It's not until I'm back in my seat having slid the simple solitaire onto Lily's finger that I take full note of Lucas.

The boy looks to be on the verge of tears, although not of happiness.

"What's wrong?" I put my hand on his back, as gently as I can, with him still wincing. Whether this is down to physical pain, or remembered pain, I'm not sure, parking it for later.

"Does this... Does this mean you don't need me... anymore?"

His words, as quiet as they've been, have still sounded loud to my ears.

"Hell no, it doesn't!" On a sharp intact of breath from Marta, I repeat myself without cussing. "Why would you think that?"

A heartbeat later and the kid is body slammed from all directions when he's dragged into what we call a family huddle.

Lily follows up on her, "Welcome to the family Lucas," by kissing him soundly on his grubby cheek. Meanwhile, I ruffle his filthy hair and tell him we're going fishing the first chance we get.

My mom, while silent, sends me a look that says she'll outfit the kid with a completely new wardrobe before the weekend is over.

It's Zoe's "A puppy!" that confuses all the adults in the room. But my daughter is right, with her now cuddling a wriggling ball of black and white fluff.

Lucas bursts into gut-wrenching sobs. "Please, can I keep him? Mr. Meadows said he'd kill him after I left."

It's yet another reason for me to want a quiet word with the asshat who's apparently made life a misery for Lucas.

"Of course, you can keep him!" says Lily. "We wouldn't be a proper family without a dog."

Never has my life felt as complete as when we drive home from social services. While Lily and I are up front, the kids are in the back, with the puppy crashed out between them.

My mom is already on her way to the supermarket, because there'll be celebrations in the Pierce/Finnegan household tonight. And with my mom's love-language being food, for the first time in a long time, Lucas won't go hungry.

THANK YOU

If you've enjoyed this story, we'd be thrilled if you could take the time to give it a rating, or even a review, before you leave. In the meantime, carry on to read more about what's coming up next.

BAD BIRDS

ALL ABOUT HOPE

Hope believes everyone deserves love, especially curvy girls. She also likes to believe there's a welcoming town like Coogan's Break for all of us. A place where the girls are curvy and the guys hotter than hell, where opposites attract, and love is steamy and fast.

www.thepapersparrow.com

LUCKY BREAK SERIES

Meet the **Lucky Break Construction** crew, whose motto should read ***"If we build it, you will come!"*** because apparently a few Coogan's Break single ladies have done just that.

Available from all good online retailers.

COOGAN'S BREAK SERIES

If you've enjoyed your time in Coogan's Break, consider staying a while, by treating yourself to the large format six packs of books 1-6 and 7-12. Available from all good online retailers.

Frankie's a jinxed witch with Bruce Lee moves.
Dex is her snarky Jack Russell. Together with Zane,
Frankie's drop-dead gorgeous, neighbor,
these three are magic.

Left in charge of her grandmother's marriage agency, vampire matchmaker, Eva De Silva, is expecting a peaceful gig. She's wrong.

On her first night, she's hit with unexpected visitors, a dangerous family relic goes missing, and she's framed for murder. Luckily, she has Dominik Zilonka—her newest client and vampire voted least likely to settle down—on hand to help.

Eva must stay sharp to save the business, clear her name, and find Dominik a wife, all while ignoring that she's his perfect blood bond.

THE PAPER
SPARROW

BUY DIRECT AND SAVE

Home to books by Andrene Low, Hope Malone, Andie Low, Sydney Hunter, and a host of others along the way.

Whether your preference is for curvy girl romances, paranormal cozies, snarky British romcoms, or something darker, we've got you covered.

Even better is that you'll enjoy discounts you might not find elsewhere.